Complete Guide To Buying A Home

Your Roadmap to Successful Homeownership

TOI HOLLIDAY

Cover design by Bjou Brzee Creations
Printed in the United States of America
First Printing: November 2023

PREFACE

Dear Home Buyer,

I feel honored and privileged that you've considered picking up my new book, "Complete Guide to Buying a Home: Your Roadmap to Successful Homeownership." Get your pen and a notebook ready because this book is more than just pages filled with advice—it's a roadmap, carefully curated to help you unlock the doors to your dream home.

I'm Toi Holliday, a dedicated real estate professional, and your guide on this journey. My roots are firmly planted in the vibrant city of Los Angeles, where I've had the privilege of witnessing countless individuals find their path to homeownership. My experiences working with diverse clients—investors, buyers, and sellers—have sculpted a profound understanding of the real estate landscape.

The heart of this guide beats with a single belief that every individual who dreams of owning a home should have the tools and knowledge to transform that dream into reality. Homeownership isn't just about having a space to call your own; it's a foundation for stability, a canvas for building family wealth, and a realization of dreams.

In my journey, I've encountered a prevailing gap—an absence of comprehensive understanding among home buyers, especially those stepping into this world for the first time.

There's often a mismatch between expectations and reality, a gap that leaves many navigating uncharted waters.

This book is my response to that challenge. It's the culmination of my experiences, lessons learned, and a commitment to ensure you, the reader, are well-equipped to make informed decisions. The goal is not just education; it's empowerment. It's about providing you with a comprehensive guide that cuts through the secrets and haze of television real estate shows and offers real, pragmatic advice for your real-life home buying journey.

Through these pages, I aim to unravel the home buying process, debunk misconceptions, and provide you with the keys to successful homeownership without the hype and glitz. Every chapter is carefully designed for easy reading to offer insight, guidance, and actionable advice, ensuring you're well-prepared for your journey.

I invite you to explore this journey with an open mind and a thirst for knowledge. I'm here to be your guide, and I'm thrilled to share this adventure with you.

Toi Holliday

TABLE OF CONTENTS

Chapter 1: Introduction to Home Buying   Page 1

Chapter 2: Assessing Your Financial Readiness   Page 5

Chapter 3: Owning vs Renting   Page 11

Chapter 4: Homebuyer Pitfalls to Avoid   Page 15

Chapter 5: Navigating The Real Estate Market   Page 20

Chapter 6: The Mortgage Process   Page 33

Chapter 7: Defining Your Ideal Home   Page 45

Chapter 8: The Home Search   Page 50

Chapter 9: 16 Ways to Buy a Home   Page 55

Chapter 10: Making an Offer and Negotiating   Page 81

Chapter 11: Home Inspections and Appraisals   Page 89

Chapter 12: The Closing Process   Page 93

Chapter 13: Homeownership Responsibilities   Page 97

Chapter 14: Post-Purchase Financial Management   Page 104

Chapter 15: Bonus Tips and Resources   Page 108

Chapter 16: Summary and Conclusion   Page 117

Additional Resources & Links   Page 121

CHAPTER 1

Introduction to Home Buying

Introduction to Home Buying

Homeownership is a milestone that ushers you into a world of opportunities, challenges, and profound financial decisions. For many, it signifies a significant investment, an emotional connection, and a symbol of accomplishment.

The Importance of Homeownership

A Place to Call Your Own

At its core, homeownership grants you the privilege of having a space you can truly call your own. It's more than just a house; it's a canvas upon which you can paint your life's story. Your choice of wall color, the arrangement of furniture, and the garden you cultivate all become expressions of your personality and aspirations.

Financial Investment

Besides the emotional benefits, homeownership represents a substantial financial investment. Real estate has proven to be a reliable wealth-building tool. As you gradually pay off your mortgage, your home typically appreciates in value, bolstering your equity.

Stability and Community

Homeownership often provides a sense of stability and community. It can be the bedrock for your family's growth and development. Children grow up in a familiar environment, you establish roots in a community, and you build meaningful relationships with your neighbors.

Why You Need This Guide

The journey to homeownership is undeniably exciting, but it's also laden with complexities. The real estate market resembles a maze; the paperwork can be intimidating, and the financial decisions are far-reaching. This is where "The Complete Guide to Buying a Home" steps in.

This guide serves as your compass through the intricate terrain of home buying. It's the trusted resource to make informed decisions, navigate the market effectively, and realize your homeownership dreams. Whether you're a first-time buyer or aiming to refine your home-buying skills, this guide is your invaluable companion.

The Versatility of Home Buying

While this guide provides comprehensive insights into various aspects of home buying, it's essential to acknowledge that the world of real estate is diverse. Numerous alternative ways to purchase a home may exist beyond the scope of this book.

Therefore, it's worth noting that this guide serves as a foundation to prepare the consumer financially, mentally, and emotionally for the home buying process. The home buyer may explore other alternative methods to purchase a home not covered here.

Setting Goals for Homeownership

Before you dive into the world of home buying, it's crucial to set clear and realistic goals. Your goals will be the guiding stars, helping you make well-informed decisions regarding the type of home you need, your budget, and the location. Ask yourself:

- Why are you considering buying a home? Is it to establish a permanent residence for your family, an investment opportunity, or a combination of both?

- What type of home suits your needs? Consider aspects like size, style, and specific features that hold significance for you.

- What is your financial capacity? Understanding your financial limits ensures you don't overextend yourself, leading to financial strain.

- Where do you envision living? Location plays a pivotal role in your home-buying decision. Consider factors such as proximity to work, schools, and essential amenities.

- What's your long-term vision? Your home-buying decision should harmonize with your long-term goals. Reflect on how this investment aligns with your life plan.

As we navigate through the chapters of this guide, we will dig even deeper into these fundamental questions and equip you with the knowledge and tools necessary to make the right choices.

The path to homeownership is as much about self-discovery as finding the right property. With "The Complete Guide to Buying a Home: Your Roadmap to Successful Homeownership " as your guide, you're well on your way to fulfilling your homeownership aspirations.

CHAPTER 2

Assessing Your Financial Readiness

Homeownership is not just about finding the right property; it's also about ensuring your financial foundation is solid. Before you step into the home buying process, it's essential to assess your financial readiness. This will guide you through the critical aspects of financial assessment to ensure you are well-prepared for the journey ahead.

Evaluating Your Financial Health

Before you start on your home buying journey, it's imperative to assess your overall financial health. Here's a step-by-step guide:

1. Review Your Credit Report: Start by obtaining a free copy of your credit report from major credit bureaus. Scrutinize it for inaccuracies, late payments, or outstanding debts. A strong credit history is vital for favorable mortgage terms.

2. Calculate Your Debt-to-Income Ratio (DTI): Your debt-to-income (DTI) ratio assesses your monthly debt obligations in relation to your income. Lenders often look for a DTI below 43%. Calculate it by adding up your monthly debt payments (e.g., credit cards, student loans) and dividing them by your monthly income.

3. Assess Your Savings: Evaluate your savings and emergency fund. Ensure you have enough for a down payment, closing

costs, and at least three to six months' worth of living expenses in case of unexpected financial setbacks.

4. Steady Employment: Lenders prefer borrowers with stable employment. Ensure you have a consistent job history or source of income.

Understanding Credit Scores

Credit scores play a pivotal role in securing a mortgage and determining the interest rate you'll receive. Here's what you need to know:

1. Credit Score Basics: Understand that credit scores typically range from 300 to 850. A higher score is favorable and indicates better creditworthiness.

2. Factors Impacting Your Score: Understand the elements that influence your credit score, including factors like your payment history, credit utilization, the duration of your credit history, the variety of credit accounts you hold, and recent credit inquiries.

3. Improving Your Score: If your credit score is less than ideal, take steps to improve it. This may include paying down debts, making on-time payments, and avoiding opening new credit accounts.

4. Monitoring Your Credit: Regularly monitor your credit reports for any discrepancies or fraudulent activity. Correcting errors promptly is essential.

5. FICO Score Requirements: Keep in mind that many down payment assistance programs may have minimum FICO score requirements, around 640. This means you need to be aware of your credit score and be prepared to meet those requirements to qualify for such programs.

Creating a Realistic Budget

To assess your financial readiness for homeownership, it's crucial to create a realistic budget. Here's how:

1. List Your Monthly Income: Start by listing your monthly income sources, including your salary, rental income, or any other sources of revenue.

2. Record Your Monthly Expenses: Categorize and track your monthly expenses, including housing costs, utilities, groceries, transportation, insurance, and discretionary spending.

3. Determine Affordability: Compare your monthly income to your expenses. Ensure that you have enough room in your budget to comfortably cover mortgage payments, property taxes, insurance, and other homeownership costs.

4. Emergency Fund: Don't forget to allocate a portion of your budget to savings, including an emergency fund, which can safeguard you against unexpected expenses.

The Role of Down Payment

The down payment is a substantial upfront cost when buying a home. Here's what you need to know:

1. Minimum Down Payment: Different mortgage programs have varying minimum down payment requirements, ranging from 0% to 20% of the home's purchase price.

2. Down Payment Sources: Understand where your down payment funds will come from. This can include savings, gifts from family, borrowing from your retirement account or down payment assistance programs.

3. Down Payment Assistance Programs: Many state and local government programs, like CalHFA (Housing Finance Agency) and GSFA (Golden State Finance Authority), offer down payment assistance to eligible homebuyers. These programs can significantly reduce the upfront financial burden, making homeownership more accessible. However, you should be aware of the small print and understand that all programs are not free, and some programs may require you to pay the money back if you decide to sale later or the program may increase mortgage points on your loan. While CalFHA and GSFA are California specific, each state in the union has a Housing Finance Agency and you should consult with a lender to discuss the details of specific programs.

4. Additional Upfront Costs: It's important to note that even with down payment assistance, you may still have some upfront expenses. These may include fees for a lender credit check, fees to participate in a home education program, closing costs or inspection related costs. Be aware of these costs as part of your financial preparation.

5. Impact on Mortgage Terms: A larger down payment often results in better mortgage terms, including lower interest rates and reduced monthly payments.

By comprehensively evaluating your financial health, understanding credit scores, creating a realistic budget, and exploring available down payment assistance programs, you'll be better prepared to make informed financial decisions on your path to homeownership. Additionally, being aware of additional upfront expenses ensures that you have a comprehensive understanding of the financial aspects of buying a home.

Buyer Financial Responsibilities During a Transaction

To ensure you're fully prepared for your new home purchase, the following list offers an overview of potential costs. It's worth noting that responsibility for some of these charges can be negotiated, and the party responsible for certain costs may vary based on your location.

✓ Title insurance premium (according to contract)
✓ Escrow fees (according to contract)
✓ General home inspection (recommended and may be required by lender or loan program)
✓ Document preparation (if applicable)
✓ Notary fees
✓ Recording charges for all documents in buyer's names
✓ Termite inspection (according to contract)
✓ Tax proration (from date of acquisition)
✓ Homeowner's transfer fee

- ✓ All new loan charges (except those required by lender for seller to pay)
- ✓ Interest on new loan from date of funding to 30 days prior to first payment date
- ✓ Assumption/change of records fees for takeover of existing loan (if applicable)
- ✓ Beneficiary statement fee for assumption of existing loan
- ✓ Inspection fees (pests/termites, roofing, property inspection, geological, etc.)
- ✓ Home warranty (according to contract)
- ✓ City transfer/conveyance tax (according to contract)
- ✓ Fire insurance premium for first year

Source: Checklist Courtesy of Lawyers Title

CHAPTER 3

Owning vs Renting

One of the fundamental decisions you'll make on your journey to homeownership is whether to own or rent a home. This chapter will explore the benefits and advantages of both options, providing you with the knowledge to make an informed choice.

The Benefits of Owning a Home

Owning a home offers several compelling advantages, and the most significant is:

1. Building Equity: When you make mortgage payments, you're not just covering the cost of your home; you're also building equity. Over time, your ownership stake in the property grows, increasing your net worth. This equity can be leveraged for future financial goals, such as purchasing a larger home, funding education, or even retirement. Building equity is a significant advantage of homeownership, as it contributes to long-term wealth and financial security.

2. Stability: Homeownership provides a stable and predictable housing cost. Unlike rent, which can increase annually, your mortgage payment typically remains consistent over the life of a fixed-rate loan.

3. Customization: When you own a home, you have the freedom to customize and renovate it to your liking. Paint the

walls, remodel the kitchen, or create the garden of your dreams; you have endless possibilities.

4. Tax Benefits: Homeowners may enjoy tax benefits, like deducting mortgage interest and property taxes. Consult a tax professional for specific details.

5. Long-Term Investment: Real estate has historically appreciated in value over the long term. Your home can be a valuable long-term investment.

The Advantages of Renting

Renting also has its unique advantages:

1. Flexibility: Renting offers more flexibility in terms of changing your living situation. You can easily relocate when your lease ends without the commitment of selling a property.

2. Fewer Responsibilities: As a renter, you're typically not responsible for major repairs or maintenance. Your landlord takes care of these issues.

3. Lower Upfront Costs: Renting requires a smaller upfront payment, primarily consisting of a security deposit and the first month's rent.

4. No Property Taxes: Renters don't have to pay property taxes.

Key Considerations: Renting or Owning

The decision to rent or own depends on various factors. To help you make an informed choice, let's explore some key considerations. Use these calculator examples to assess the financial aspect of both options:

1. Rent vs. Buy Calculator: This tool assists you in evaluating the expenses associated with renting as opposed to purchasing a home. It considers factors like your monthly rent, potential home price, down payment, mortgage rate, and the length of time you plan to stay in the home. It can provide a clear financial picture of which option is more cost-effective over a specified period.

2. Mortgage Affordability Calculator: If you're leaning towards homeownership, this calculator helps you determine how much house you can afford. It considers your income, down payment, mortgage rate, and other financial factors to provide an estimate of the home price within your budget.

3. Equity Calculator: This tool estimates your ownership in a property by subtracting the outstanding mortgage balance from its current market value. This calculation offers insights into your financial stake and wealth-building potential in homeownership.

3. Long-Term Financial Goals: Consider your long-term financial goals and how homeownership or renting aligns with them. Think about factors like investment strategies, retirement plans, and overall financial stability.

By thoroughly evaluating these factors, utilizing the provided calculators, and ensuring that your housing choice aligns with your financial objectives, you can make an educated choice on whether to rent or purchase a home. This choice is a significant one, and taking the time to evaluate all factors is essential for your financial well-being. Building equity through homeownership is a substantial advantage, ensuring long-term wealth and financial security.

Calculators

Rent vs Buy Calculator
https://bit.ly/RentvsBuy_TH

Scan QR code ➤

Mortgage Affordability Calculator
https://bit.ly/LoanAffordability-TH

Scan QR code ➤

Equity Calculator
https://bit.ly/CheckMyEquity-TH

Scan QR code ➤

CHAPTER 4

Homebuyer Pitfalls to Avoid

Buying a home is a significant life event that can be both exhilarating and emotionally challenging. In this chapter, we'll explore the importance of cultivating the right mindset and readiness to navigate the home-buying journey successfully. We'll also discuss setting realistic market goals, the potential dangers of overspending, and the significance of addressing any emotions that may arise during this process.

Home Buyer Mindset and Readiness

The home-buying process is not just a financial transaction; it's a journey that often stirs a range of emotions. To approach it with the right mindset:

1. Alignment of Goals: Ensure that all decision-makers involved in the home purchase are aligned with the same goal. This involves open and honest communication about expectations, budgets, and priorities.

2. Flexibility: Be prepared to remain flexible throughout the process. The real estate market can be dynamic, with shifts in interest rates and housing inventory. Having flexibility is essential to embrace the ever-changing market.

3. Mental and Emotional Preparedness: Understand that unexpected situations can arise. Whether it's a sudden market change or unexpected repairs during a home inspection,

mental and emotional preparedness will help you handle these situations with resilience.

4. Financial Capability: Be cautious not to overspend. Set a clear budget and stick to it. Avoid extending yourself beyond your financial capability, as this can lead to financial strain.

5. Rent vs. Mortgage: Be aware that your monthly mortgage payment could potentially exceed your current rent. This shift is an investment in your future. Buying a home builds legacy wealth while paying rent merely supports someone else's mortgage. Understand that building equity is a long-term financial strategy.

Managing Home Buyer Emotions

Buying a home can evoke a range of emotions, including fear, excitement, and uncertainty. It's essential to address these emotions:

1. Fear: Fear of making a significant financial commitment is natural. Seek support from financial advisors or professionals who can provide guidance and alleviate your fears.

2. Excitement: Balance your excitement with rational decision-making. Avoid making impulsive decisions based solely on emotions.

3. Uncertainty: Uncertainty is common in any life-changing event. Seek clarity through communication with real estate professionals and thorough research.

4. Visualization: Take some time to visualize your ideal home. Envision the layout, the design, and the atmosphere. This visualization can help you keep an eye out for properties that align with your desires.

5. Mindfulness: Participating in mindfulness techniques can be a valuable method for handling stress and anxiety during the home-buying process. It can provide mental clarity and a sense of calm that is beneficial when making critical decisions.

6. Buyer's Remorse: Understand that buyer's remorse is a common emotion after a significant purchase. It's the feeling of regret or anxiety about the decision. Acknowledge it, but also remind yourself of the careful considerations and planning that led to your choice. If the feeling persists, discuss it with your real estate agent or seek advice from professionals to address concerns and make informed decisions.

Cultivating the right mindset, being financially prepared, setting realistic goals, avoiding overspending, and addressing your emotions are essential steps in your home-buying journey. With the right approach, you can navigate this process with confidence and ensure that your first home purchase is a significant step towards building your financial future and legacy wealth.

Setting Realistic Market Goals

Setting realistic market goals is essential to avoid disappointment and frustration. Consider the following:

1. Market Analysis: Perform comprehensive market analysis to grasp the current conditions. Determine whether it's a buyer's or seller's market, as this can impact your expectations.

2. Budget: Establish a budget that aligns with your financial readiness. This budget should encompass not only the purchase price but also associated costs like property taxes, insurance, and maintenance.

3. Priorities: Revisit your list of must-have and nice-to-have features. Focus on your priorities to ensure that you are searching for a home that meets your essential needs.

4. Long-Term Vision: Think about your long-term goals. Consider how this home fits into your overall life plan and whether it has the potential for future equity growth.

Dangers of Overspending

Overspending can have long-term financial consequences. Avoid these potential pitfalls:

1. Sticking to Your Budget: Your budget is a guideline for a reason. Stick to it to ensure that you don't overextend yourself financially.

2. Avoiding Impulse Purchases: Be cautious of impulsive decisions, especially when emotions are running high. It's easy to be swayed by a property that exceeds your budget, but this can lead to financial strain.

3. Consider All Costs: Remember that homeownership comes with additional expenses like property taxes, insurance, maintenance, and unexpected repairs. These costs should be factored into your budget.

CHAPTER 5

Navigating The Real Estate Market

Comprehending the dynamics of the real estate market is an essential aspect of your path to homeownership. This chapter will provide a comprehensive view of how to research housing markets, choose the right neighborhood, work with real estate agents, and utilize online resources effectively.

Researching Housing Markets

Researching housing markets is an essential first step in the home-buying process. Here's how to do it effectively:

1. Market Trends: Keep an eye on market trends in your desired area. Look for patterns in home prices, supply and demand, and the average time properties spend on the market. This data can help you understand whether it's a buyer's or seller's market.

2. Local Economic Factors: Examine local economic factors, such as job growth, industry presence, and infrastructure development. These factors can impact housing market stability and future property values.

3. Property Appreciation: Research historical property appreciation rates in your chosen area. Doing so can provide insights into potential long-term investment opportunities.

Choosing the Right Neighborhood

Selecting the right neighborhood is a critical decision in the home-buying process. Consider these factors:

1. Proximity to Work: Evaluate the commute to your workplace and ensure it aligns with your lifestyle and daily routines.

2. Schools and Education: Research local schools to see if you have children or plan to in the future. High-quality schools can impact property values.

3. Amenities and Services: Consider access to amenities like parks, shopping centers, healthcare facilities, and recreational activities.

4. Safety and Security: Investigate the safety and crime rates in the neighborhood. Online resources and local law enforcement agencies can provide this information.

5. Future Development: Look into potential future developments or infrastructure projects that may impact the neighborhood.

Understand How to Work With Real Estate Agents

Before we delve into the importance of working with a real estate agent, we must highlight two crucial distinctions in the real estate industry: Real Estate Agent vs REALTOR® and Client vs Customer.

Real Estate Agent vs. REALTOR®: Real estate agents may vary in their qualifications and commitments; starting with the difference between a REALTOR® and a real estate agent who is not a REALTOR®. REALTORS® are real estate agents who also maintain membership in the National Association of

REALTORS® (N.A.R.). These agents have taken an oath to adhere to strict codes of ethics and are held to high professional standards. Both can assist you in buying a home, the choice between the two is your decision based on the level of service and commitment you seek.

Client vs Customer:

According to the National Association of REALTORS®, a "client" means the person(s) or entity(ies) with whom a REALTOR® or a REALTOR®'s firm has an agency or legally recognized non-agency relationship. A "customer" means a party to a real estate transaction who receives information, services, or benefits but has no contractual relationship with the REALTOR® or the REALTOR®'s firm.(1)

As a client, the real estate agent has a contractual obligation to adhere to fiduciary duties, commitment, and confidentiality and provide a higher level of dedicated and catered services outlined in a Buyer's Agency Representative Agreement. As a customer, the real estate agent does not have a contractual obligation to adhere to fiduciary duties, commitment or provide the level of dedicated services the agent is bound to according to a Buyer's Agency Representative Agreement.

Choosing to be a customer may result in a lower level of attention, leading to possible confusion about responsiveness or the lack of certain exclusive services or receiving detailed property information from agents. Understanding the implications of this choice is vital to align the level of service with your home-buying needs. While services might be limited to a customer, real estate agents and REALTORS® are bound to treat each client and customer fairly, honestly, and abide by all state and federal laws.

Moreover, it's essential to emphasize the significance of effective communication when selecting an agent. Don't simply choose an agent because of a personal connection; opt for one with the skills and knowledge to guide you through the home-buying process successfully. Consulting with a real estate professional will clarify their range of services, ensuring you find the right match for your home-buying journey.

The Value of Working with a Real Estate Agent

Now, let's explore why having an agent to represent you is vital in the home-buying experience. However, before delving in, there are key insights that can significantly aid your approach:

Knowledge and Expertise: A seasoned agent's wealth of experience and comprehensive understanding of the home buying process are invaluable. From navigating negotiations to unraveling complex contracts, their guidance is pivotal. They empower you to make well-informed decisions and provide access to an extensive network of viable resources. This network includes established connections with vendors you'll need during and proceeding with your transaction, home buyer programs, relationships with lenders to ensure you have the necessary tools and understanding to navigate the complexities of buying a home.

Access to Listings: Real estate agents are gatekeepers to many property listings. Access to the Multiple Listing Service (M.L.S.) offers a comprehensive selection of properties even before they appear on public platforms. Moreover, agents often have access to 'coming soon' or off-market properties. 'Coming soon' listings provide a preview of properties about to hit the market, while off-market or pocket listings offer a more discreet sales approach. This insight into off-market properties is particularly appealing to sellers who prioritize confidentiality. The landscape of real estate regulations often changes, so it's recommended to check with a real estate agent regarding off-market properties in your area.

Property Tours and Showings: Agents take care of all the scheduling and provide access to properties. They obtain detailed information about the properties and find out the sellers' expectations, enhancing your overall home-buying experience.

Negotiation Skills: Navigating negotiations in the real estate realm demands a skilled hand. A proficient agent serves as your advocate, adeptly negotiating on your behalf. Their expertise in handling price discussions, contingencies, and property repairs ensures the best possible deal for you.

Contracts and Disclosures: Agents play a crucial role in helping buyers understand the complex world of contracts and disclosures. They decipher legal language, explain terms, and ensure that you comprehend the implications of each document. This expertise helps you make informed decisions and mitigates the risk of misunderstandings during the transaction.

Transaction Management: Real estate transactions involve many details that require meticulous management. Your agent provides detailed guidance through the entire sales transaction, overseeing the preparation and timely submission of all required documents. They act as a central point of contact, streamlining communication between all parties involved.

Escrow and Title: Agents play a crucial role in coordinating with escrow and title services. They ensure that the necessary paperwork is processed efficiently, facilitating a smooth transfer of ownership.

Inspection and Repairs Request Management: From scheduling inspections to negotiating repairs, your agent manages the entire process. They help you navigate through inspection reports, advising on necessary repairs and negotiating with the seller on your behalf.

Loan and Appraisal: Your agent collaborates with lenders to ensure a seamless loan application process. They assist in gathering necessary documentation and facilitate communication between you, the lender, and other parties involved. Additionally, they help address appraisal-related concerns.

Final Walkthrough: Before closing, your agent will accompany you on the final walkthrough to ensure that the property's condition aligns with your expectations. Any last-minute issues can be addressed before completing the transaction.

Closing and Post-Closing: During the closing, your agent ensures that all required documents are signed and submitted. Post-closing, agents provide valuable resources for local utility companies in the neighborhood, guiding you on transferring or setting up essential services such as water, electricity, gas, and internet. Additionally, they offer assistance in addressing any lingering concerns, ensuring a seamless transition into your new home.

In summary, a real estate agent's multifaceted role extends far beyond being a mere intermediary. Their knowledge, access to listings, and negotiation proficiency are essential components that significantly influence the success of your home-buying journey.

Buyer's Agency Representation Agreement

A Buyer's Agency Agreement formalizes the buyer's and agent's partnership, elevating you to a represented client. This contract defines the agent's responsibilities and the buyer's obligations, ensuring transparency and mutual protection.

Understanding the importance of a signed buyer agency agreement is crucial. Without this formal commitment, the level of protection and dedicated representation from a real estate agent might not be assured. The absence of such an agreement could position you merely as a customer, potentially missing out on the agent's formal commitment, confidentiality, or exclusive fiduciary duty in prioritizing the buyer's best interests. This scenario can vary based on legal regulations and practices that differ from one location to another.

Notably, each agent adheres to a unique standard of practice, and it remains at their discretion whether they require prospective buyers to sign a buyer's agency representation agreement. Engaging in a comprehensive discussion with your real estate agent is vital to clarify these specifics and to gain a complete understanding of the local laws governing agency relationships.

Cancellation of the Buyer's Agency Agreement

There might arise situations where canceling a buyer's agency agreement becomes necessary. Understanding the cancellation process is crucial in case of dissatisfaction with the provided services. Ordinarily, buyers can cancel the agreement in writing any time before an offer is written and or accepted. However, before proceeding with the cancellation, engaging in open communication with your agent is advisable to address any misunderstandings or unresolved concerns. Familiarizing yourself with local regulations or seeking legal guidance is essential as, in certain circumstances, terminating the agreement might result in potential liability to pay commissions to the agent's brokerage. This situation arises when a buyer bypasses the agent and purchases the property through another agent, which the current agent was actively assisting with, constituting a breach of contract.

Fiduciary Duty and Buyer's Agent Responsibilities

Both listing agents, representing the seller and the buyer's agents, have distinct fiduciary duties. Listing agents are legally bound to secure the best possible deal for the seller while maintaining confidentiality. Simultaneously, buyer's agents are committed to protecting the buyer's interests, ensuring confidentiality, and advocating for the best terms and price. Engaging a dedicated buyer's agent who diligently works for you is ideal to safeguard your interests. Some states restrict listing agents from simultaneously representing both the buyer and seller due to potential conflicts of interest. These states include Alaska, Colorado, Florida, Kansas, Maryland, Texas, Wyoming, and Vermont. However, an agent from the same office might be able to represent the other party. It's recommended for buyers to acquaint themselves with their local guidelines in this regard.

Myth of Directly Approaching the Listing Agent

A common misconception prevails that directly approaching the listing agent guarantees a superior deal. However, it's essential to recognize that the primary loyalty of the listing agent is to the seller. Their obligations are firmly bound by the listing agreement and the seller's instructions. Revealing confidential or sensitive information about the seller's financial situation or "bottom line" could potentially breach their fiduciary duty. The listing agent's responsibility is to present all offers to the seller, ensuring the best possible outcome, ultimately aiming to create a win-win situation for both the seller and buyer. Thus, approaching the listing agent directly does not always ensure a more advantageous deal for the buyer. Regardless of whom you choose to collaborate with, it's crucial to ensure that your interests are prioritized and negotiated appropriately.

Navigating Dual Agency Representation: In some states, a single agent may represent both the seller and buyer in a transaction, known as dual agency representation. Effectively managing this requires maintaining strict confidentiality between both parties. It's essential to consider potential conflicts of interest in this scenario thoroughly. It is strongly recommended to engage in detailed discussions with your real estate agent to employ a comprehensive understanding of guidelines and best practices regarding dual agency.

Understanding How Agents Get Paid

When you engage the services of a real estate agent, it's essential to be aware of how their compensation works. Typically, real estate agents earn a commission based on the final sale price of the property. This commission is negotiable and can vary, but it is often around 2-6% of the home's sale price.

Here are key points to keep in mind:

1. Seller Pays Commission: In most cases, the seller agrees to pay the commission for both the listing and buyer's agents according to the Cooperative Compensation Rule (depending on your jurisdiction).

2. Negotiation of Commission: The commission percentage is not fixed and can be negotiated. Both buyers and sellers can discuss this with their respective agents.

3. Buyer Incentives: Buyer's agents may offer incentives or buyer credits; this is a deduction from their commission—it is not required, nor should it be expected for agents to give a portion of their paycheck to a client or customer.

4. Transparency: Have an early, transparent discussion with your agent about commissions. Understand the structure and services covered. See diagram below.

Sample Commission Breakdown
(Seller Pays Listing Side 4% Total, it's split with the Buying Side)

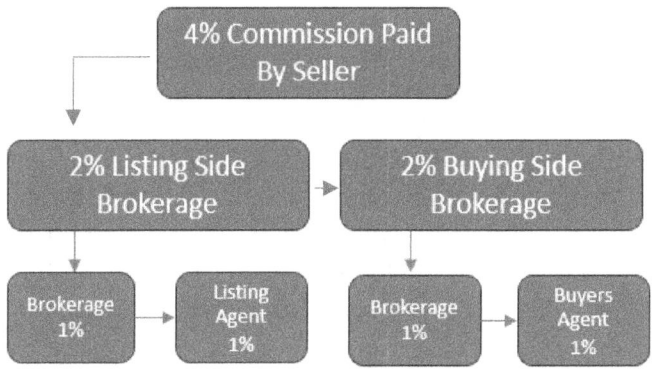

While the presented breakdown serves as an example, it's important to note that commission structures can differ among brokerages. It's essential to understand that the commission paid by the seller to the listing brokerage does not influence the value of the property. The value of a property is determined by various factors, such as its condition, features, location, size, and prevailing market trends. Following the sale of the property, the seller receives a net amount representing the remaining proceeds after covering all associated fees.

Buyers need to be aware of this - when a seller does not agree to collaborate on compensation for the buyer's agent, the buyer may assume responsibility for the commission – this is especially important when buyers reach out to agents requesting an agent to start search for off market or for sale by owner properties where there is no agreement. Therefore, a thorough understanding of commission structures ensures a transparent and informed process for buyers and sellers.

Understanding How a Buyer's Premium Work

Unlike traditional transactions where the seller covers the real estate agent's commission, online auctions may charge the buyer a Buyer's Premium.

What is a Buyer's Premium?

A buyer's premium is an additional fee, usually as a percentage of the winning bid (3% to 5%), that the buyer pays on top of the final sale price. This premium goes to the auction platform and the seller and is a common practice in online real estate auctions.

Transparency is Key:

Before starting in an online real estate auction, review the auction terms and conditions carefully to understand the buyer's premium details. Transparency is essential to make informed decisions about your budget and overall investment.

Consult with Your Real Estate Agent:

Given the nuances of online auctions and the buyer's premium, consulting with your real estate agent is strongly advised. They can provide insights into structuring your offer appropriately, considering this extra fee and ensuring a transparent and successful bidding experience.

Online Resources for Home Searching

In today's digital age, online resources play a significant role in home searching. Here's how to make the most of them:

- Real Estate Websites: Utilize real estate websites and apps to search for properties, view photos, and access property details.
- Virtual Tours: Many listings offer virtual tours, allowing you to explore properties from the comfort of your home.
- Local Property Portals: Check local property portals for listings that may not be available on larger platforms.
- Email Alerts: It is easy to sign up for email alerts on real estate websites to receive notifications about new listings and price changes that match your criteria.

By conducting thorough research on housing markets, choosing the right neighborhood, and working with a qualified real estate agent, you'll be well-prepared to navigate the real estate market with confidence. Remember, your buyer's agent is your advocate, and their expertise is invaluable in securing the best possible deal and guiding you through the complexities of the home-buying process.

Sources: (1) https://www.nar.realtor/about-nar/governing-documents/code-of-ethics/2023-code-of-ethics-standards-of-practice

CHAPTER 6

The Mortgage Process

The mortgage process is a fundamental aspect of buying a home. It's not just a step; it's the heartbeat of your home purchase. From understanding various mortgage types to navigating through the difference between pre-approval and final approval, we explore the impact of interest rates on your loan, unravel the complexities of mortgage closing costs, and shed light on current loan limits. However, it's crucial to highlight a fundamental truth: your active participation and financial readiness in this process are non-negotiable. Without being preapproved or showing another means to make your home purchase, essentially stalls you from moving forward. As a result, making offers on potential properties without this crucial step is null and void. So, let's get started on the process.

Types of Loans

There are various types of mortgage loans to consider, each tailored to different circumstances:

1. Conventional Mortgage Loans: These are standard loans not backed by any government agency. They typically require higher credit scores and are sometimes called nonconforming loans.

2. FHA (Federal Housing Administration) Mortgage Loans: Designed for low-to-moderate-income borrowers, these loans have lower down payment requirements and more flexible credit score criteria.

3. FHA 203(k) Rehab Loans: These loans enable buyers to finance both the purchase of a home and the cost of rehabilitation or renovation with a single mortgage.

4. VA (Veterans Affairs) Mortgage Loans: Exclusive to eligible veterans, these loans offer low or no down payment options and competitive interest rates.

5. USDA (US Department of Agriculture) Loans: Tailored for homebuyers in rural and suburban areas, providing low or no down payment alternatives for eligible properties.

6. Foreign National Loans: Foreign national loans cater to non-U.S. citizens looking to purchase property in the U.S. Some lenders offer specialized loans with different documentation and down payment requirements. Additionally, the EB-5 Immigrant Investor Program, a visa investment program, allows eligible foreign investors to apply for a U.S. visa by investing a specific amount of capital in real estate or in a new commercial enterprise that will create jobs in the U.S.

7. Adjustable-Rate Mortgages (ARM): These loans have an initial fixed-rate period, after which the interest rate adjusts periodically based on market conditions.

8. Fixed-Rate Mortgages: These loans offer a stable interest rate over the life of the loan, making budgeting predictable.

9. Conforming vs. Nonconforming Mortgages: Conforming loans meet specific requirements set by Fannie Mae and Freddie Mac; these loans present a maximum on how much you can borrow. While nonconforming loans do not adhere to these guidelines, and the borrower can borrow into the millions for a home - also known as Jumbo Loans.

10. Length of Mortgages: You have options like 15-year, 30-year, and even 40-year mortgage terms, each with its implications for interest and monthly payments.

11. Loans for 1099 Self-Employed: Lenders offer specialized loans for self-employed individuals, considering income documentation variations.

12. Non-QM (Non-Qualified Mortgage) Loan: A Non-QM loan is a type of mortgage that doesn't meet the qualified mortgage standards set by regulatory agencies. These loans often cater to borrowers with non-traditional financial situations, providing more flexibility in eligibility criteria.

13. Hard Money Loan: Hard Money loan is a short-term, asset-based loan secured by real estate. These loans are provided by private investors or companies and are based on the property's value rather than the borrower's creditworthiness. They are often used for real estate investments or in situations where traditional financing is challenging to obtain.

14. Current Loan Limits: Keep in mind that there are loan limits that can impact the maximum amount you can borrow for specific loan types. These limits can change, so it's essential to stay informed about the most recent figures. As of January 1, 2023, loan limits for conforming loans (Federal Housing Finance Agency, Fannie Mae, and Freddie Mac) are $726,000 for most of the USA and $1,089,000 in high-cost markets such as San Francisco and New York (1). Some lenders have raised their conforming loan limits to $750,000 for 2024, offering a 3.2% increase from the current limit of $726,000 (2).

Pre-Approval vs. Final Approval

Understanding the difference between pre-approval and final approval is vital:

Pre-Approval: Getting pre-approved is crucial for understanding your buying power early in your home search. It is the responsibility of the buyer to be actively engaged in this process, meeting minimum requirements by providing accurate and complete financial information. This proactive approach ensures a realistic understanding of loan eligibility, streamlining the overall home buying process.

Final Approval: This is the last step in the mortgage process, where the lender verifies all your information and approves your loan. It typically occurs after you've chosen a specific property and you've entered the escrow phrase. However, some lenders have the ability to underwrite your home loan to make the closing process go much faster.

Lender Required Documents: Your lender must verify and validate your ability to repay the home loan. You should be prepared to provide your lender with proof of income and proof of employment. The following documents may be requested - W-2, 1099, recent bank statements, Tax Returns, employment verification from your employer, and recent check stubs. Each lender has its own set of guidelines, but these are the primary documents required for a new home loan, unless you work with lender who offers "Stated Income" loans.

How Interest Rates Affect Your Loan

Interest rates play a pivotal role in shaping your mortgage

experience. It's essential to understand the different types of interest rates and their effects on your loan:

Fixed Interest Rates: With fixed interest rates, your mortgage rate remains constant throughout the life of your loan - in the event rates adjust downward you can always consider refinancing for lower monthly payments. However, having a fixed interest rate loan can provide predictability in your monthly payments. You'll always know exactly how much you need to budget for your mortgage, making it easier to plan your finances.

Adjustable Interest Rates (ARM): On the other hand, adjustable interest rates may change periodically, influencing your monthly payment. These rates can fluctuate with market conditions, and it's crucial to comprehend how these changes work and how they can impact your budget.

Homebuyers need to consider that the level of interest rates directly affects their monthly payment. Higher interest rates can drive up the amount you pay each month. Keep in mind, attempting to time the market or forecast interest rates is a highly unpredictable endeavor.

The right time to buy a home is often when you, as the buyer, are ready. Whether interest rates are high or low, life events continue to unfold. Job opportunities and relocations, expanding families, marriages, divorces, downsizing, and the basic desire to upgrade to larger homes are all part of life's journey. Regardless of interest rate fluctuations, life events will persist and the best time to buy is when you are ready.

One aspect for buyers to consider is that when interest rates are higher, there may be less competition in the real estate market; properties stay on the market a little longer and sellers are open to negotiate and possibly offer credits towards closing costs. In such scenarios, lenders often offer programs to assist buyers in mitigating the impact of higher interest rates. These programs, such as buydown options, can make homeownership more attainable and help alleviate the financial burden of increased interest rates.

Ultimately, buying a home should align with your circumstances, goals, and readiness. Don't let the unpredictability of interest rates deter you from securing the home of your dreams when the time is right for you.

Strategic Approaches to Lowering Mortgage Costs

A 3-2-1 or 2-1 buydown is a financing arrangement that lowers the initial interest rate on a mortgage for a specified period. This is often used to make the loan more appealing to borrowers, especially when interest rates are rising. Here's how it works:

3-2-1 Buydown: For those looking for even more favorable terms, the 3-2-1 buydown is an option that lets buyers pay less interest on their mortgage for the first three years of the loan. By paying points upfront, the interest rate is reduced by 1% for each of those initial three years.

2-1 Buydown: A 2-1 buydown offers homebuyers a unique opportunity to enjoy a reduced interest rate during the initial two years of their mortgage. In the first year, the interest rate is lowered by a substantial 2%, followed by a 1% reduction in the second year. See illustration in diagram #1.

Consider a 2-1 Buydown!

Buy this house with a **5.25%** interest rate instead of 7.25%!

	1st Year	2nd Year	3-30 Year
Sales Price:		$500,000	
Loan Amount:		$450,000	
Interest Rate:	5.25%	6.25%	7.25%
Monthly PITI:	$3,237	$3,522	$3,821
Monthly Savings:	**$585**	**$299**	-

Using the $10,607 seller credit to lower your rate would be equal to **$110,000 more in buying power!** *near it*

Diagram #1: 2-1 Buydown sample

As seen in diagram #1, the primary aim of a buydown is to provide borrowers with a lower interest rate at the beginning of the loan. This can result in more affordable monthly mortgage payments, making homeownership accessible. This is particularly advantageous for borrowers who anticipate future income growth and prefer lower initial payments. The difference between the reduced initial rate and the standard interest rate is typically covered by the seller, builder, or borrower, depending on the agreement.

Buydowns are frequently applied to fixed-rate mortgages, and the specific terms can vary based on the lender and the loan program. It's crucial to carefully review the buydown agreement's terms, including who is responsible for covering the additional interest cost during the buydown period.

In a buydown scenario, buyers can bring additional money to the table to buy down points. If not, buyers may contemplate negotiating for a seller credit into their offer; this is typically done by slightly increasing your offer to cover the credit amount you want to ask the seller for - this seller credit will help offset the cost of buying down the interest rate. This strategic approach can make homeownership more affordable in the long run. The seller credits can be applied to the extra interest cost during the buydown period, easing the financial burden on the buyer during the initial mortgage years. The feasibility of such negotiations may depend on the transaction's terms and the seller's willingness to provide buyer credits. It's essential for buyers to discuss these options with their real estate agent and lender for strategic negotiations.

Mortgage Closing Costs

Mortgage closing costs are expenses incurred when the home purchase is finalized:

Common Closing Costs: These may include fees for appraisal, title search, escrow services, taxes, attorney's services, home warranty, and more.

Understanding Closing Costs: Being aware of these costs and budgeting for them is essential to avoid unexpected financial surprises at the closing table. By not understanding your responsible obligations when it comes to closing costs can make or break walking into your new home.

When starting a successful home purchase, it's important to have a comprehensive understanding of the mortgage process, the various types of loans available, the importance of pre-approval, and the implications of interest rates and closing costs, including the impact of current loan limits on your borrowing capacity. This understanding enables you to make well-informed choices and secure the appropriate mortgage for your home.

Understanding Private Mortgage Insurance (PMI)

Private Mortgage Insurance, often known as PMI, functions as a protective measure for lenders in cases where borrowers provide a down payment less than 20% of the property purchase price. PMI is a common component of many mortgage loans and plays a crucial role in facilitating homeownership, especially for those who may not have the means to provide a substantial down payment.

How PMI Works:

1. Protection for Lenders: PMI protects the lender, not the borrower. It's designed to mitigate the risk associated with lending to buyers with smaller down payments. In other words, if a borrower defaults on their loan, the PMI policy reimburses the lender for the financial loss incurred.

2. When PMI Is Required: Typically, PMI is required when the down payment is less than 20% of the home's purchase price. This is often the case with conventional loans, especially for first-time homebuyers.

3. Cost of PMI: The expense of PMI can vary based on elements like the loan amount, down payment percentage, and credit score. PMI fees are generally included in the borrower's monthly mortgage payment.

4. Cancelling PMI: The good news for borrowers is that PMI is not a permanent expense. Once the equity in the home reaches 20% or more, borrowers can usually request the

cancellation of PMI. This can be achieved through a combination of making regular mortgage payments and potentially making additional principal payments to build equity.

5. Options to Avoid PMI: If you'd like to avoid PMI altogether, consider options such as securing a loan with a 20% or higher down payment, looking into loan programs that don't require PMI, or exploring alternatives like government-backed loans with their own insurance programs.

Understanding how PMI functions is essential for buyers who plan to make a smaller down payment. It's a financial instrument that enables numerous individuals to access the real estate market without necessitating a significant upfront investment. However, it's important to recognize that PMI comes with an additional cost, so weighing the pros and cons and knowing how to manage PMI is a key aspect of responsible homeownership.

Mortgage Life Insurance: Protecting Your Home and Loved Ones

Buying a new home is a significant financial undertaking, and one of the utmost priorities in homeownership is securing your investment and your family's future. Mortgage Life Insurance is a valuable tool designed to provide peace of mind in the event of unforeseen circumstances.

What Is Mortgage Life Insurance?

Mortgage Life Insurance, often referred to as Mortgage Protection Insurance, is a specialized insurance policy intimately connected to your mortgage. Its primary purpose is to ensure that your mortgage is paid off in full if you, as the homeowner, pass away during the term of the policy.

How Does Mortgage Life Insurance Work?

Here's how Mortgage Life Insurance typically functions:

1. Policy Coverage: When you purchase a Mortgage Life Insurance policy, you select the coverage amount. This amount is usually equivalent to the outstanding balance on your mortgage.

2. Premium Payments: You pay regular premiums for the policy. These premiums are often included as part of your monthly mortgage payment, simplifying the process. You can also acquire mortgage life insurance from an independent insurance company.

3. Beneficiary: You designate a beneficiary, usually a family member or someone with an insurable interest in your mortgage. In the unfortunate event of your passing, the insurance pays out the policy amount directly to your beneficiary.

4. Mortgage Payment: Your beneficiary can use the insurance payout to pay off the remaining mortgage balance. This can assist in guaranteeing that your family can maintain residence in their home without the added financial strain of mortgage payments.

Advantages of Mortgage Life Insurance:

Security for Your Family: Mortgage Life Insurance provides financial protection for your family, allowing them to stay in their home and maintain their quality of life.

Debt Elimination: It ensures that your mortgage is paid off, relieving your family of a significant financial obligation.

No Medical Exam: In many cases, Mortgage Life Insurance is available without the need for a medical exam, making it accessible to a wide range of individuals.

Considerations:

Premium Costs: The cost of Mortgage Life Insurance can differ based on factors like your age, health, and the outstanding balance on your mortgage. It's essential to understand the premium costs and ensure they fit within your budget.

Coverage Limitations: While the insurance pays off the mortgage, it may not provide additional financial support to your family. It's crucial to evaluate your family's overall financial needs.

Mortgage Life Insurance is a valuable resource for homeowners aiming to safeguard their family's financial well-being in case of their passing. Yet, it's crucial to evaluate your unique situation, including your family's financial needs and budget, to determine whether Mortgage Life Insurance aligns with your objectives. Seek advice from a licensed Mortgage Life Insurance specialist to make an informed decision.

Source:
(1) Source: https://singlefamily.fanniemae.com/originating-underwriting/loan-limits
(2) https://www.forbes.com/advisor/loans/advisor-mortgages-advisor-mortgages-lenders-raise-loan-limits/

CHAPTER 7

Defining Your Ideal Home

When starting on the journey to homeownership, one of the first and most critical steps is defining your ideal home. In this chapter, we'll guide you through the process of setting realistic expectations, differentiating between your needs and wants, setting priorities, and creating a homebuying checklist.

Understanding that your first home can be a steppingstone to future financial growth is key.

Defining the Type and Style of Home

When crafting your vision of the ideal home, it's crucial to consider the property type that best suits your lifestyle and future aspirations, as well as the architectural style that resonates with you. Here are some common property types to contemplate:

1. Single-Family Homes: These standalone structures offer independent living and often include yard space. They can be detached or attached to neighboring homes, sometimes termed as townhouses in many cities.

2. Condominiums: These units are part of larger complexes and often include shared amenities. Condos might involve homeowners' association (HOA) fees for maintenance and community services.

3. Townhouses: Attached single-family homes with multiple floors and shared walls in a row.

4. Income Properties: Options like duplexes, triplexes, or fourplexes provide rental income. These properties fall within the range of being considered a single-family home with two, three, or four separate units.

Architectural Style Consideration

Alongside the property type, consider the architectural style that aligns with your preferences. Whether it's Victorian, Colonial, Craftsman, Modern, Contemporary, or any other style, your architectural preferences play a significant role in finding a home that matches your aesthetic and lifestyle.

By understanding the type and style of home that best aligns with your needs and preferences, you'll refine your search and enhance the likelihood of locating a property that suits your lifestyle and fulfills your home-buying goals.

Needs vs. Wants

It's essential to distinguish between your needs and wants when searching for a home:

1. Needs: These are the essential features and qualities that your home must have to meet your basic requirements. For example, the number of bedrooms and bathrooms needed for your family, proximity to work or schools, and safety considerations are typically classified as needs.

2. Wants: Wants are features or amenities that would be nice to have but are not absolutely essential. These can include a

gourmet kitchen, a large backyard, or a swimming pool. While they can enhance your lifestyle, they should be weighed against your budget and overall priorities.

Setting Priorities

Setting priorities is crucial, especially if you have a limited budget:

1. Budget: Begin by determining your budget. This should include the purchase price and factors like property taxes, insurance, and ongoing maintenance costs.

2. Must-Have Features: Identify the features and attributes that you consider non-negotiable. These are your needs.

3. Nice-to-Have Features: List the features you would like but can live without if necessary. These are your wants.

4. Future Considerations: Think about your long-term goals. If you plan to expand your family or work from home, these considerations should be factored into your priorities.

Realistic Goals for Your First Home

Understanding that your first home doesn't have to be your forever home. Here's why:

Building Equity: Your first home serves as the foundation for accruing equity. Over time, this equity can pave the way for potential upgrades, profitable sales, or utilizing it as leverage for a second home purchase, enabling you to secure a more substantial property.

HELOC and Investment: With the equity accrued from your first home, you can explore options like a Home Equity Line of Credit (HELOC) to fund a second home purchase, home improvements, or the addition of an ADU (Accessory Dwelling Unit). This approach can transform your first home into an investment, generating a steady monthly income.

Flexibility is Key: Your first home holds the potential to evolve along with your changing needs. Whether converting an office into an additional bedroom, transforming a garage into a home gym, or renovating spaces to increase value, your initial property can adapt to suit your lifestyle. If the preferred type of home isn't within your current budget, keeping an open mind regarding different property types or exploring nearby cities and towns could expand your options.

Creating a Homebuying Checklist

To guide your search and ensure you find a home that aligns with your needs and priorities, create a homebuying checklist:

1. Location: Determine your preferred neighborhoods, considering factors like proximity to work, schools, and amenities.

2. Budget: Clearly define your budget, including your maximum purchase price and any potential financial considerations.

3. Must-Have Features: List the non-negotiable features your home must have to meet your basic requirements.

4. Nice-to-Have Features: Enumerate the features you would like but can live without if necessary.

5. Long-Term Goals: Think about your future goals, such as family expansion, potential home improvements, or investment opportunities.

6. Pre-Approval: Get pre-approved for a mortgage, so you'll know your buying power and can act quickly when you find the right property.

By setting realistic expectations, distinguishing between needs and wants, setting priorities, and understanding the potential of your first home as a financial steppingstone, you'll be well-prepared to embark on your home buying journey. Keep an open mind about your future needs and the adaptability of your first home, and you'll be on your way to finding a property that suits your lifestyle and financial goals.

CHAPTER 8

The Home Search

The home search phase is undoubtedly one of the most exciting parts of the home-buying process. However, it's crucial to approach it with practical strategies and a clear understanding of your budget and expectations. In this chapter, we'll explore effective house-hunting strategies, how to make the most of home tours and open houses, and the importance of taking notes and making comparisons to ensure you find the best value.

Effective House-Hunting Strategies

When starting your home search, it's essential to have a strategy in place:

1. Purchasing Budget: First and foremost, stay within your budget. If you have a $500,000 budget, don't waste time looking in areas where properties typically sell for $880,900. Being realistic about what you can afford is essential to avoid disappointment and time wasted.

2. Location Considerations: Focus on areas that align with your financial plan and way of life. Take into account aspects such as distance to your workplace, schools, and nearby conveniences. This approach will assist in streamlining your property search.

3. Agent Expertise: Rely on the expertise of your real estate agent. They can provide guidance and insights into neighborhoods and properties that align with your budget and preferences.

4. Property Priorities: List your property priorities, including the number of bedrooms and bathrooms, essential features, and any specific criteria that matter to you.

Home Tours and Open Houses

Home tours and open houses are opportunities to explore potential properties. Here are a few tips to consider for home tours and open houses:

1. Respect for Properties: Show courtesy during property visits. Keep in mind that you are a visitor in someone else's residence. If requested, remove your shoes, refrain from handling personal belongings, and adhere to any guidance given by the listing agent.

2. Surveillance Cameras: While touring someone else's home, it's essential to be aware that many homeowners have surveillance cameras installed within the property. This means that your actions during the tour might be under surveillance and recorded. It's important to respect the homeowner's privacy and act accordingly during the tour.

3. In-Depth Inspection: Pay close attention to the property's condition. Check for signs of wear and tear, potential maintenance issues, and the overall quality of the home.

4. Ask Questions: During home tours or open houses, be proactive in asking specific questions about the property. Focus on practical details such as the age of appliances and recent renovations. While it's important to gather information, be mindful that personal circumstances affecting the seller, such as a sudden job loss, death in the family, or health-related reasons don't directly influence the value of the property. Some buyers attempt to exploit these situations to make low-ball offers targeting potentially desperate sellers, which is an unfair tactic in the buying process. Be mindful of the questions you ask and be cautious with the information you share.

5. Take Notes: Making notes is crucial during home tours. Jot down your impressions, likes, and dislikes for each property. This will help you make informed decisions when it's time to choose.

Open houses are complimentary events that provide an excellent opportunity for potential buyers to explore homes on the market. They serve as a source of inspiration as you refine your preferences and requirements for your new home. Attending open houses independently during the browsing phase allows you the freedom to gather initial impressions.

As you progress from the browsing phase to serious consideration, it's advisable to involve your real estate agent when attending open houses. Having your agent accompany you serves multiple purposes. They can engage in face-to-face conversations with the seller's representative, gaining insights into the details of the house and the seller's expectations. This collaboration ensures that you have professional support in understanding the property's nuances and negotiating effectively when you're ready to make an offer.

Making Comparisons and Taking Notes

Making comparisons and taking notes is a fundamental part of your home search:

1. Comparative Market Analysis: Collaborate with your real estate agent to perform a Comparative Market Analysis (CMA) on the properties that pique your interest. A CMA offers valuable data on fair market values, helping you avoid overpaying.

2. Evaluation Criteria: Create a set of criteria to evaluate each property. Consider factors like location, property size, condition, and features. This will help you objectively compare your options.

3. Pros and Cons: List the pros and cons of each property. Be as objective as possible. Consider both the emotional and practical aspects of the property.

4. Prioritization: Once you've viewed several properties, prioritize your favorites based on your criteria and notes. This will help you narrow down your choices and make an informed decision.

By following these effective house-hunting strategies, respecting properties during home tours, and making detailed notes and comparisons, you'll be well-prepared to find the perfect home that aligns with your budget and preferences.

Remember that your real estate agent is a valuable resource throughout this process, helping you make informed decisions and ensuring you get the best value for your investment..

CHAPTER 9

16 Ways to Buy a Home

In this chapter, we'll take a look at a variety of home-buying methods, providing you with a wealth of information on each approach and the steps to successfully navigate the routes to homeownership. It's important to note that there are numerous ways to purchase property, but our focus in this chapter will be on examining 16 specific methods for buying a home. Whether you're interested in traditional options, unconventional strategies, or government programs, our goal is to offer you a comprehensive understanding of the choices at your disposal.

1. Traditional Purchase

Overview: The traditional purchase method, as discussed in the preceding chapters, involves buying a home through the standard process. This typically includes securing a mortgage loan and making a down payment. This method is the most common and well-known approach to homeownership.

Steps:
1. Financial Preparation: Review your finances, assess your credit score, and save for a down payment or search for down payment assistance programs.

2. Get Pre-Approved: Consult with mortgage lenders to get pre-approved for a loan, which helps determine your budget.

3. House-Hunting: Start your home search by finding a real estate agent to help you locate properties within your budget and based on your preferences.

4. New Construction or Resale: Decide whether you prefer a brand-new home or a resale property with a history and character.

5. Make an Offer: When you find a suitable home, make an offer, including the proposed purchase price and terms.

6. Negotiation: Negotiate with the Seller regarding the price and terms of the sale.

7. Offer Acceptance: Seller will either accept, reject or counter your offer. Once your offer is accepted, the Seller will open escrow.

8. Earnest Money Deposit: Respond to all correspondence from the escrow officer and wire your deposit to escrow within 3 days after your offer being accepted (or timeline in your agreement).

9. Home Inspection: Arrange a home inspection to identify any potential issues with the property.

10. Appraisal: The lender orders an appraisal to ensure the property's value aligns with the loan amount.

11. Finalize Loan: Finalize all loan requirements with your lender.

12. Closing: Sign the necessary documents and finalize the purchase.

The traditional purchase method is a tried-and-true approach to homeownership, offering a structured path to acquiring a home. Whether you're a first-time homebuyer or an experienced one, understanding this method is essential for making informed decisions on your journey to homeownership. This method provides a solid foundation for the subsequent chapters, which explore unconventional methods that can broaden your perspective on acquiring a home.

2. Rent-to-Own

Overview: Rent-to-own or lease-to-own agreements allow renters to gradually transition into homeownership.

Steps:
1. Search for Rent-to-Own Homes: Find properties with owners open to rent-to-own agreements.

2. Negotiate Terms: Discuss the lease period, monthly rent, and purchase price with the property owner.

3. Sign a Lease-Option Agreement: Execute a lease-option agreement outlining the terms and the option to purchase the property.

When exploring Rent-to-Own or Lease Option programs, buyers have various avenues to consider, including private sellers and dedicated programs. Rent-to-Own programs can be an excellent choice for individuals who believe that rent-to-own is the ideal path to homeownership. One key advantage of rent-to-own is that it allows buyers to "try before they buy," giving them the opportunity to experience living in the property before committing to ownership.

However, it's important for buyers to be aware that some Rent-to-Own programs may elevate the price of the property when selling it to you.

Understanding Rent-to-Own Programs:

It's essential to understand that in Rent-to-Own or Lease Option programs, you function as a tenant, and your name will not appear on the property title. The Seller retains full ownership rights until the end of your term, should you choose to purchase the home. Before proceeding with this option, consider asking the Seller the following questions:

1. Responsibility for Repairs: Clarify who will be responsible for necessary repairs, including plumbing, roofing, electrical malfunctions, and major maintenance issues that may arise.

2. Allocation of Monthly Payments: Determine whether your monthly payments contribute to the property's purchase or if a portion goes towards your down payment.

3. Purchase Price Timing: Inquire if the purchase price will be based on the market value when you initially signed your lease option agreement or if the purchase price is based on the market value at the time of purchase.

3. Seller Financing

Overview: Owner or seller financing, also known as seller carryback, is an alternative method of purchasing property where the property seller acts as the lender, simplifying the financing process for buyers. These methods are particularly useful when traditional financing is challenging to obtain.

Steps:
1. Negotiate with the Seller: When exploring owner financing, start by discussing the sale price, down payment, interest rate (if any), and repayment schedule with the property owner.

2. Create a Financing Agreement: Draft a formal financing agreement that outlines the terms and conditions of the arrangement. This document will serve as the legal basis for the transaction.

3. Monthly Payments: In owner financing, you will make monthly payments to the property owner as per the agreement until the property is paid off.

Seller financing may necessitate a higher down payment from the buyer, which typically falls within the range of 20% to 50% of the purchase price. The specific amount can vary based on local practices and the type of property being purchased directly from the seller. It's important to keep in mind that sellers are not financial institutions, so they tend to prefer shorter loan terms.

As a result, seller financing contracts are often structured for relatively brief periods, typically spanning 18 to 36 months, with a fixed interest rate. When this term concludes, the buyer might be required to refinance the property to settle the remaining balance with the seller, or they may face a balloon payment, which means paying off the outstanding balance in full. Surprisingly, in some cases, the interest rates offered through seller financing can be lower than those available from traditional banks.

These methods offer an alternative path to homeownership, simplifying the financing process by working directly with the Seller. It's highly advisable to seek guidance from legal and financial professionals to ensure that the agreement's terms and conditions are equitable and aligned with your specific needs.

4. Auctions

Overview: Home auctions present an alternative avenue for acquiring property, presenting distinctive opportunities alongside potential challenges. It's crucial to understand that numerous auctions, particularly public events like Trustee's Auctions, Sheriff's Auctions, or Tax Auctions, often don't permit visual interior inspections before bidding and also may necessitate cash payments.

Prospective buyers should exercise caution and adhere to the guidelines and restrictions set by the auction organizers. Some auctions, like those involving government surplus properties, may allow for drive-by inspections and even taking photographs from the curb, but it's vital to respect the rules and regulations. Walking onto a property without permission can be considered trespassing and may result in legal consequences, such as fines and even imprisonment, depending on the jurisdiction. Thus, it's essential to be prepared for these particular aspects.

Steps:

1. Research Auctions: Begin by identifying upcoming home auctions and the properties they feature. Make sure to review the auction details, including the date, location, property listings, available photos if available and the investigative due diligence period.

2. Bid on Properties: When you've found properties of interest, register, and actively engage in the auction by placing your bids. It's important to establish a budget and adhere to it, considering that auctions can become highly competitive. Be mindful that there may be a required deposit before bidding on a property, typically ranging from $250 to $5,000, depending on the type of auction and jurisdiction.

3. Winning the Bid: If your bid is the winning one, congratulations! You'll need to complete the purchase by fulfilling any requirements outlined in the auction terms. This might involve providing a cash payment or meeting other specific conditions. Be sure to understand and adhere to these requirements to secure your purchase successfully.

Auctions provide a unique and exciting way to acquire a property, but it's essential to thoroughly research and prepare for the specific auction you plan to attend. Understanding the payment requirements and auction rules is crucial for a smooth and successful experience.

5. Co-Buying: A Joint Path to Homeownership

Overview: Co-buying, also known as Joint Homeownership or Co-Ownership, is a strategy where multiple individuals (two or more) come together to jointly purchase a property. This method has become very popular in the last ten years with rising home prices but offers a unique opportunity for prospective homeowners to share the financial burden and responsibilities of property ownership. Whether you're considering Co-Buying with a family member, friend, or even a co-investor, it's essential to understand the process and potential challenges.

Steps:
1. Partner Selection: Choose your Co-Buying partners wisely. This step involves finding like-minded individuals who share your homeownership goals and financial commitment.

2. Financial Arrangements: Clearly define each Co-Buyer's financial responsibilities, including the initial investment, ongoing mortgage payments, property maintenance, and any potential profit-sharing agreements. Consider consulting with a legal professional to draft a Co-Buying agreement that outlines the financial arrangement and responsibilities in detail.

3. Property Search: Collaborate with your Co-Buyers to identify suitable properties within your collective budget. Ensure that the chosen property aligns with everyone's preferences and requirements.

4. Financing: Secure a mortgage that accommodates Co-Buyers. Mortgage lenders have specific requirements for Co-Buying arrangements, and you'll need to provide all necessary documentation to qualify for the loan.

5. Legal Counsel: It's highly advisable to consult with an attorney experienced in real estate and Co-Buying agreements. This legal professional can draft a legally binding agreement that addresses various scenarios, including exit strategies if one Co-Buyer wishes to sell their share.

6. Co-Buying Agreement: The Co-Buying agreement should detail property ownership percentages, how expenses will be divided, procedures for selling or transferring ownership, and dispute resolution mechanisms. This document is crucial for protecting each Co-Buyer's interests.

7. Ongoing Communication: Open and transparent communication is vital in a Co-Buying arrangement. Regular meetings or discussions should address financial matters, property maintenance, and any concerns that may arise.

Co-buying offers unique benefits, such as shared financial responsibility, which can make homeownership more affordable. However, it's essential to consider potential challenges, such as disagreement among Co-Buyers and the need for a well-structured Co-Buying agreement. Additionally, the resale of a Co-Bought property may require agreement from all Co-Buyers.

By pursuing the Co-Buying journey, you and your Co-Buyers can work together to achieve homeownership goals while sharing the responsibilities and joys of owning a property.

6. Government Programs

Overview: The government offers various programs and initiatives to make homeownership more accessible, often providing unique opportunities for specific demographics or individuals in need of affordable housing solutions. These programs can be invaluable for prospective homebuyers looking for alternative paths to owning a home.

Steps:
1. Research Eligibility: Determine if you qualify for specific government programs. Explore various programs, including:

   a) HUD's Dollar Homes Program: This initiative from the Department of Housing and Urban Development (HUD) offers the opportunity to purchase homes for just $1 in certain communities. It aims to revitalize neighborhoods and provide affordable housing options.

   b) Good Neighbor Next Door: This program is designed for law enforcement officers, teachers, firefighters, and emergency medical technicians. It offers substantial discounts on homes in revitalization areas.

   c) USDA Rural Development Programs: The USDA offers various programs to assist individuals in rural and suburban areas. These initiatives include loans, grants, and other resources to promote homeownership.

d) State and Local Housing Programs: Many states and local governments have their own homeownership programs, which may provide down payment assistance, grants, or reduced interest rates to cater to specific needs of their communities. Contact your local housing.

e) Land Banks and Blighted Property Programs: In some areas, government and state agencies operate land banks or maintain lists of blighted properties. These initiatives focus on the revitalization of neighborhoods and can offer opportunities to purchase properties directly from the state or county. Research your local area to find such programs, which aim to transform blighted properties into thriving, affordable homes. Remember, some of these statewide programs may require cash, and financing may not be an option.

2. Apply for Assistance: Once you've identified a program that suits your circumstances, follow the application process outlined by the respective program. This typically involves submitting the necessary documentation and adhering to program-specific requirements.

3. Comply with Program Requirements: Ensure that you meet all program requirements, including income limits, property eligibility, and any other criteria set by the program. Carefully review each program's terms and conditions to understand the benefits and obligations.

Government homeownership programs are designed to break down financial barriers and make owning a home a reality for a wider range of individuals. They can be particularly advantageous for those with limited resources or specific needs.

These programs contribute to the stability and vitality of housing markets and communities, offering unique opportunities to individuals who might not otherwise be able to afford a home. Exploring these options and understanding the available benefits can be a significant step toward your goal of homeownership.

Note: Government programs may evolve or change over time, so it's essential to stay updated on the latest offerings and eligibility requirements in your area. Consult with local housing agencies, real estate professionals, and government resources for the most current information.

7. Government Agency Surplus Properties

Overview: Government agency surplus properties, including those from agencies like the General Services Administration (GSA), Department of General Services (DGS), Department of Transportation, and more, can offer unique opportunities for homebuyers.

Steps:
1. Research Government Surplus Properties: Begin by researching surplus properties available from government agencies at the federal, state, or local level. Explore listing auction platforms or contact these agencies directly to find out the requirements and qualifications in order to purchase properties from

them. Be aware that some agencies may require you to be an established business supporting housing or homeless initiatives in order to participate in their surplus property programs. Understanding these requirements is crucial before you proceed.

2. Auction Participation: Many governments' surplus properties are sold through auctions. Familiarize yourself with the auction process, including registration, bidding, and payment procedures.

3. Inspect and Verify (if possible): Before committing, try to thoroughly inspect the property. Keep in mind that some surplus properties may be sold "as is" with limited or no inspection access. It's important to be aware that bids on these properties are often "as is" and "sight unseen." Buyer beware.

8. Tax Defaulted or Tax Deed Properties

Overview: Purchasing properties through tax auctions, resulting from the failure to pay property taxes, can offer real estate at a lower cost. However, navigating the complexities of tax auctions requires an understanding of the unique considerations and potential challenges involved.

Steps:
1. Research Tax Auctions: Begin by identifying tax auctions where properties are available due to tax delinquency. It's important to note that, in many cases, you may not have the opportunity to inspect the property before placing your bid, which adds an extra layer of risk to the process.

2. Redemption Period: Familiarize yourself with the local laws governing the period during which the property owner may redeem the property. For guidance, consider contacting the local tax assessor's office or seeking advice from a legal representative specializing in tax-defaulted property sales.

3. Participate in the Auction: Attend the auction or sign up for the online auction platform and engage in the bidding process. While tax auctions can be open to the public, they often require cash payments, so it's essential to be prepared with the necessary funds.

4. Complete the Purchase: If you secure the winning bid, you must fulfill all requirements and payments outlined in the auction terms. Conduct thorough due diligence before bidding to understand the guidelines and conditions. Keep in mind that some auction platforms may necessitate a deposit to bid. If you do not secure a property then your deposit will be returned to you.

Additionally, it's crucial to be aware that each state has distinct statutes and redemption periods, so thoroughly familiarize yourself with the state-specific regulations before participating. While investing in tax-defaulted properties can be a promising endeavor, it's vital to recognize the unique risks involved and proceed with caution, backed by comprehensive research.

9. Inheritance

Overview: Acquiring a home through inheritance, either from a family member's will or from a Family Trust when someone passes away.

Steps:

1. Legal Processes: Understand and navigate the legal procedures related to inheritance, which may involve probate or trust administration. Consult with an estate attorney to ensure you follow all legal requirements.

2. Assess Property: Make sure the property gets appraised. Evaluate the condition and market value of the inherited property. This step is essential to understand what you're acquiring.

3. Ownership Transfer: Complete the necessary paperwork to transfer the property into your name, following the legal procedures applicable in your jurisdiction.

Acquiring a home through inheritance can be a straightforward process, especially in states where real estate agents may not be required for property transfers in such cases. You can obtain regular financing to purchase an inherited home. However, it's crucial to familiarize yourself with local jurisdiction laws and seek the guidance of an estate attorney. Additionally, negotiating with the designated trustee of the estate can help streamline the process.

It's worth noting that buyers may choose to obtain a loan to purchase an inherited property, making homeownership achievable even in the context of inheritance. This allows individuals to continue a family legacy and create a home filled with cherished memories.

10. Leased-Land Properties

Overview: Leased-land properties involve leasing the land to build a home while typically owning the house situated on it. This arrangement provides more affordable homeownership options, allowing you to own a home that might otherwise be beyond your budget. Common examples include manufactured homes or properties in areas with reservations. Leased-land properties often come with lower upfront costs compared to traditional homeownership. However, there are potential drawbacks, such as escalating lease payments and challenges when selling the home.

Steps:
1. Understanding Lease Arrangement: Recognize that in leased-land properties, you own the house but lease the land it's located on. This can be an economical way to become a homeowner, but it's crucial to understand the unique terms of your lease.

2. Foreclosure and Liens: If you default on land lease payments, the landowner has certain rights. The leasehold lender can foreclose, similar to a traditional mortgage. However, during foreclosure, the interest being sold is the ground lease and its associated rights, not the land itself. The lender's claim is limited to the leasehold interest, not ownership of your house.

3. Surrender Clause: Pay close attention to the surrender clause in your lease agreement. This clause outlines what happens if the lease expires while you still own the house. Depending on the terms, you may need to remove your house from the leased land or negotiate a new lease.

4. Types of Land Leases: Two primary types of land leases exist: subordinated and unsubordinated. With a subordinated land lease, the landowner is at risk if the tenant defaults on their property loan. The lender could claim the land along with the property. An unsubordinated land lease keeps the land and property separate, reducing such risks.

5. Due Diligence: When considering a leased-land property:

6. Look for keywords like "manufactured home" or "leasehold interest" in property listings.

7. Investigate hidden facts and understand the unique features of this type of homeownership.

8. Be aware of potential steep homeowners' association (HOA) fees associated with leased-land properties.

Remember that while leased-land properties offer affordability, they come with specific risks. Always consult legal professionals and thoroughly understand your rights and obligations before entering into such arrangements.

11. House Hacking

Overview: House hacking involves purchasing either a single-family property or a multi-unit property and residing in one of the units or bedrooms while renting out the other units or bedrooms to offset your mortgage expenses. It's a creative way to achieve homeownership while generating rental income.

Steps:
1. Identify a Property: Begin your house hacking journey by searching for properties in your desired area.

2. Secure Financing: Apply for financing appropriate for multi-unit properties, such as an FHA loan, which offers favorable terms for owner-occupants.

3. Live in One Unit/Bedroom: Choose one of the property's units or bedrooms to be your home while renting out the remaining spaces.

4. Manage the Property: Oversee the rental units, handle maintenance, and manage tenants to ensure a smooth and profitable housing arrangement.

Note: If you decide to house-hack a single-family home, be sure to check with your local jurisdiction for any legal requirements related to minimum days of tenant occupancy. Some areas may have regulations regarding the minimum length of time a tenant (or guest) may stay, especially if you plan to utilize short-term rentals. In such cases, a license or registration may be required by the city.

House hacking is a flexible and innovative approach to homeownership that can significantly reduce your housing costs and help you build wealth through rental income. Whether you're interested in a single-family property or a multi-unit dwelling, this strategy can be a steppingstone to achieving your homeownership goals. Lastly, you want to familiarize yourself with local tenant and landlord laws.

12. Subject-to Purchase

Overview: In a subject-to-purchase, the buyer acquires a property "subject to" the existing mortgage, taking over the loan without formally assuming it. This method can be a way to purchase properties with favorable financing terms.

Steps:
1. Identify Subject-to Properties: Look for properties with existing mortgages where sellers are open to subject-to purchases.

2. Negotiate the Deal: Discuss the terms, the mortgage transfer process, and any associated costs with the Seller.

3. Transfer the Mortgage: Work with the Seller to transfer the existing mortgage into your name and ensure compliance with lender requirements.

Consult with local legal experts who can guide you through this process to ensure you understand the process before attempting this strategy.

13. Assumption Purchase

Overview: An assumption purchase involves taking over an existing mortgage, typically requiring formal approval from the lender to assume the loan.

Steps:
1. Find Assumption Properties: Seek properties with assumable mortgages and confirm that the lender allows assumptions.

2. Negotiate with the Seller: Discuss the terms, the assumption process, and any financial arrangements with the Seller.
3. Gain Lender Approval: Work with the lender to complete the assumption process, ensuring all lender requirements are met.

There are several platforms online you can research to find possible assumption purchases. Investors who use this strategy are able to locate prospective sellers who are under financial duress or facing foreclosure.

14. Buying Land and Building a Home

Overview: Another approach to homeownership is to purchase land and construct your own house. While this method provides the freedom to design and build your dream home, it also comes with unique challenges and considerations.

Steps:
1. Research and Financing: Before embarking on this journey, research the available financing options. Not all banks offer construction loans, so it's essential to find a lender that specializes in new construction home loans.

2. Construction Loan Types: Some banks may require you to purchase the land separately and then finance you for construction of the home. Research and select a construction loan type that suits your needs.

3. Buying the Land:

a) Online Searches: You can begin your search by exploring online listings. Many real estate websites and platforms provide information on available land for sale. This is a convenient way to get an overview of what's on the market.

b) Auctions: Attend land auctions in your area, which can sometimes provide opportunities to purchase land at competitive prices. Be sure to research and understand the auction process before participating.

c) Local Exploration: Another approach is to physically visit the neighborhoods where you envision building your home. This not only allows you to explore potential areas but also gain a firsthand sense of the community.

d) Developer Offerings: In some cases, developers offer lots within a tract before construction begins. This approach can benefit both buyers and developers, as it helps secure funds for the upcoming construction. Be sure to consider these options if you find a development project that aligns with your preferences.

e) Prefabricated or Manufactured Homes: You might also explore options with builders of prefabricated or manufactured homes. Some of these builders offer financing packages that cover both the land purchase and the construction of the new home. However, as with any significant financial commitment, thorough research and a clear understanding of the terms are crucial.

Before making any decisions, conduct due diligence and ask pertinent questions to ensure that your land purchase aligns with your goals and budget. Each option may have specific terms and considerations, so understanding these details is vital to making an informed choice on your path to building your own home.

4. Pre-Construction Costs: Understand that pre-construction costs are costs relevant to non-tangle items not related to the cost of materials and labor. These costs can sometimes be substantial depending on various factors such as jurisdiction, zoning, size, and shape of the land and what you plan to build. An example of these expenses include:

   - Feasibility Studies
   - Architectural Designs and Drawings
   - Soils Test
   - Environmental Reports
   - Land Survey, Slope Survey, Site Survey
   - Permits & Planning
   - Utility Installation
   - Contract Fees

5. Consult with Professionals: Engage with licensed professionals who can provide guidance through the planning and design phase and help you manage these costs effectively. Your local real estate agent may have referrals for local builders and other professionals who can help you through the process of buying land and building a home on it.

6. Zoning and Residential Conversion: Before finalizing your decision, confirm that the chosen land is

appropriately zoned for residential use or has the potential for conversion to residential development. This step is crucial for understanding the legal aspects of building your home on the selected property. Keep in mind that different jurisdictions may have restrictions on factors like the size and type of homes allowed per acre or lot. It's important to note that the purchase of vacant land doesn't automatically grant unrestricted building rights, which means you may face limitations on constructing structures like tiny houses or living in your mobile home trailer. To ensure a smooth process, proactively engage with the local planning authority to gain clarity on the permissible construction options for your potential vacant land purchase.

7. Timelines and Approvals: Be prepared for varying timelines in the construction process. The duration can range from a few months to several years, depending on your jurisdiction's approval of plans, issuance of permits, and reaching the "Ready to Issue" (RTI) stage. These timelines can significantly impact your project, so it's important to be patient and plan accordingly.

Building your own home offers the opportunity to create a personalized living space tailored to your preferences. However, it requires diligent research, a clear financial strategy, and collaboration with professionals who can navigate the complexities of land acquisition and new construction. As you explore this avenue, keep in mind that thorough planning and preparation are essential to a successful project.

15. REO/Bank-Owned Properties

Overview: Real Estate Owned (REO) or bank-owned properties are homes that have been foreclosed upon and are now owned by banks or financial institutions as a result of not selling during the foreclosure process. This section explores the process of purchasing such properties.

Steps:
1. Identifying REO Properties: Start your search for REO (Real Estate Owned) properties in your desired area. You can explore the available listings on real estate websites, reach out to local real estate agents, or directly contact banks that may have REO properties for sale.

2. Property Inspection (if possible): If property inspections are permitted, it's wise to thoroughly assess the property's condition. Keep in mind that REO properties are typically sold "as is-where is," which means the buyer should expect no repairs or credits. In many cases, banks utilize asset management teams who collaborate with local real estate agents to facilitate the sale of these properties. Contact your agent or the agent representing the bank to inquire about the possibility of inspecting the property before submitting your offer. This step can provide valuable insights into the property's condition and help you make an informed decision.

16. Probate Properties

Overview: Buying a home through probate can be a unique opportunity, but it comes with its own set of considerations. Probate properties are often sold when someone passes away, and their assets, including real estate, need to be distributed as part of the estate settlement.

Steps:
  1. How to Find Probate Properties:

    a) Newspaper Ads: Start by checking local newspapers or online listings for estate sales or probate auctions. These advertisements may feature properties for sale.

    b) Real Estate Agent: Consider working with a real estate agent experienced in probate properties. They can help you identify potential listings and guide you through the process.

    c) Courthouse Visit: Visit your local courthouse or county records office to access probate records. Look for upcoming sales or properties in the probate process.

    d) Probate Attorneys: Contact probate attorneys who may be aware of properties in the estate settlement process. They can provide valuable insights into potential probate property listings. Be aware that attorneys do exercise client confidentiality and you may not be able to obtain specific information about a property.

  2. Making an Offer:

Once you've identified a probate property you're interested in, you can make an offer. Keep in mind that the executor or administrator may not know the property's condition or have detailed information about it.

If the executor has full authority, they can choose to sell the property with or without a real estate agent. They can accept an offer they deem suitable to settle the estate's affairs.

If the executor or administrator doesn't have full authority, the offer may need to be approved by the probate judge. This means that on the court date, the property becomes open to the public, and someone may attend and outbid your offer.

Navigating the purchase of a home through the probate process can be a unique and potentially cost-effective opportunity. However, it's crucial to note that probate laws may vary based on your jurisdiction. Despite potential variations, the process for finding probate properties generally remains the same. To ensure a smooth experience, it's essential to understand the specific probate laws in your area and be prepared for the unique challenges associated with this method.

CHAPTER 10

Making an Offer and Negotiating

Making an offer on a property is where the journey to homeownership truly takes shape. It's a significant step that requires a clear understanding of the market, contracts, and negotiation skills. In this chapter, we'll explore the art of making a strong offer, comprehending contract terms, mastering the art of negotiation, and effectively handling counteroffers.

Crafting a Strong Offer

A strong offer is essential to secure the home you desire:

1. Market Value: Ensure your offer aligns with the property's market value. Rely on your real estate agent to provide a detailed comparative market analysis (CMA). This analysis helps prevent overpaying or buying a home above its appraised value. It's essential not to depend solely on online estimates, known as AVMs (Automated Valuation Models), to determine your home's worth. AVMs generate estimates based on available system data without considering homes in a side-by-side comparison.

However, in competitive markets with limited supply and extremely low interest rates, such as during the 2020-2021 pandemic, it's common for buyers to exceed the appraised value. If necessary, thoroughly discuss this decision with your lender and real estate agent. Determine the potential pros and cons to ensure the added cost is manageable and truly justified.

2. Contract Terms: Carefully craft the terms of your offer, including the purchase price, contingencies, and timelines. Make sure your offer reflects your commitment and ability to meet these terms. Keep in mind that your real estate agent cannot tell you what your offer price should be, they can only make recommendations based on market trends and the price you want to offer is your ultimate decision.

3. Contingencies: Contingencies protect your interests by providing you with opportunities to inspect the property, secure financing, and address any issues. Be sure to include the necessary contingencies in your offer.

Opening Escrow

When your offer is accepted, the next step in the process is the seller opening escrow. Escrow is a critical phase in a real estate transaction where a neutral third party is responsible for holding and disbursing the funds. Additionally, the escrow officer assists in the finalization of the transaction and records the sale with the county recorder's office.

Please note that the specific procedures related to escrow may vary depending on your jurisdiction.

Escrow Process: Once an escrow opens, the home buying process accelerates. As a rule of thumb, escrow periods commonly last 30 days or as outlined in the purchase agreement. During this time, there will be many moving parts, and the process will start to speed up, much like a moving locomotive.

Deposit of Earnest Money: Upon opening escrow, you typically have a specific timeframe to place your good faith or earnest money deposit into the escrow account. This deposit is a demonstration of your commitment to purchasing the property and is usually outlined in the purchase agreement. The specific terms, such as the amount and timeline, should be detailed in your contract. Typically, you have 3 days, or as specified in the purchase agreement, to get your earnest money deposited into escrow from the date of offer acceptance. The deposit is an essential part of the transaction and serves to secure your interest in buying the property. If you do not deposit your earnest money according to the terms outlined in your purchase agreement, you may find yourself in breach of contract and the seller has every right to issue a cancellation of the sale to you. You should consult with your real estate agent for additional guidance.

During the escrow period, several critical tasks must be completed simultaneously:

- Due Diligence: Buyer Investigation period also known as due diligence, is outlined for a period of 17 days (or the number of days in your agreement) after the date your offer is accepted. What this means is that you have 17 days to investigate whatever you need regarding the property. This may include ordering inspections, checking for code violations, property permit statuses, reviewing seller disclosures, and reviewing the preliminary title report.

- Property Inspection: This includes ordering inspections to identify any potential issues with the property. It's essential to thoroughly review the inspection reports once you receive them and address the concerns promptly. Your real estate agent will assist you in addressing any potential issues and follow up with the seller's agent promptly. Refer to the chapter on Home Inspections and Appraisals.

- Loan Approval: Simultaneously, you'll need to finalize any loan requirements within 21 days or less – this involves the final steps of the lender's underwriting process (employment verification, verifying down payment funds, etc).

- Appraisal: The lender orders an appraisal to verify the value of the property and to ensure you are not paying more for the property than it's worth. This step is vital to secure the financing needed to purchase the home. An appraisal is typically completed in 21 days or less.

- Home Insurance: During this parallel process, your lender will request you to obtain quotes for home insurance and select a suitable carrier. Home insurance is a crucial safeguard for your investment and is typically mandated by the lender. Be sure to collect quotes and opt for a carrier that offers the appropriate coverage for your new home.

- Contingency Removal: As inspections, appraisals, loan approvals, and home insurance are finalized, you'll need to remove contingencies per the terms of your contract. This signifies your commitment to the purchase.

These steps will run in parallel, and staying on top of them is crucial to ensuring a smooth and successful escrow process. If you are working with a real estate agent, they will help you efficiently manage these tasks, which will ultimately lead to securing the home you desire.

Understanding Contract Terms

Understanding contract terms is crucial to navigating the legally binding aspects of the home purchase:

1. Legally Binding: A real estate contract is a legally binding agreement. When you sign, you commit to fulfilling your end of the deal. Failure to do so may result in losing your deposit.

2. Contingencies and Timely Removal: Contingencies are specific conditions outlined in the contract that protect your interests. It's not enough to be aware of these contingencies; you must also promptly remove them after each phase of the transaction. For example:

- Buyer Inspection Contingency: After the inspection is completed, the buyer must promptly inform the seller of their satisfaction with the outcome. If issues are identified, the buyer can request repairs or a credit to cover necessary fixes.
- Loan and Appraisal Contingencies: These contingencies must also be removed in a timely manner. Failing to do so or not responding promptly can put your deposit at risk.

3. Dates and Timeframes: Contract terms include specific dates and timeframes for various aspects of the purchase. Make sure you're aware of these deadlines and adhere to them to avoid complications. Prompt and efficient removal of contingencies is vital to keep the transaction on track and protect your deposit.

The Art of Negotiation

Negotiation is a delicate process that can turn your offer into a win-win situation:

1. Flexibility: Embrace flexibility during negotiations, recognizing that sellers, like buyers, have their financial considerations. While it's common for buyers to seek repairs and seller credits, it's crucial to understand that sellers may face constraints in accommodating every request. Sellers might have financial obligations, such as a mortgage balance, other liens, property transfer taxes, insurances, and closing costs, including commissions. To foster a positive negotiation process, it's essential to be realistic and flexible in your requests. Entrust your real estate agent to navigate this sensitive phase, aiming for a win-win outcome for both parties.

2. Win-Win: Approach negotiation with the goal of creating a win-win situation. If you truly love the property, be open to making concessions that benefit both parties. This approach fosters positive negotiations and increases your chances of success.

3. Effective Communication: Clear and concise communication is key in negotiation. Be respectful and diplomatic in your interactions with the seller and their agent. This may help build rapport and lead to a smoother transaction.

Handling Counteroffers

Counteroffers are common in the negotiation process:

1. Assessing Counteroffers: When you receive a counteroffer, carefully assess it. Consider the changes in price, terms, and any conditions or contingencies the seller may introduce.

2. Response Strategy: Determine your response strategy. You can accept the counteroffer, reject it, or submit a counter-counteroffer. Identify your options with your real estate agent to make an informed decision.

3. Timely Responses: Keep in mind that time is often of the essence in real estate transactions. Promptly respond to counteroffers to keep the negotiation process moving forward.

By crafting a strong offer that aligns with market value, understanding contract terms, mastering the art of negotiation, and effectively handling counteroffers, you'll be well-prepared to navigate this critical phase of the home-buying process. Keep an open mind for win-win negotiation strategies that can lead to a successful transaction and help you secure the home you desire.

Additional Considerations: Buyer Beware

When making an offer on a property, it's crucial to be aware of the principle of "buyer beware." Homes are typically sold in an "as-is" condition, which means that the seller is not obligated to make any repairs or improvements to the property. While this can be advantageous for sellers, as it simplifies the transaction, it places a significant responsibility on the buyer to conduct proper investigations before moving forward.

Here are key points to keep in mind:

As-Is Condition: In many real estate transactions, the property is sold in its current condition, and the seller is not required to fix any issues or offer warranties. This is why the adage "buyer beware" is so important. It underscores the need for thorough property inspections and due diligence.

Property Inspections: To protect your interests, you should always consider conducting comprehensive property inspections, even for newly constructed homes. These inspections can reveal any hidden defects, structural issues, or necessary repairs. If issues are identified, you can either negotiate with the seller to address them, accept the property as-is with the knowledge of these issues, or, in some cases, choose not to proceed with the purchase.

Disclosure Laws: While homes are typically sold as-is, there are disclosure laws in place in many jurisdictions. Sellers may be required to disclose known issues with the property. Be sure to review local laws and regulations to understand what sellers are obligated to disclose in your area.

Negotiation: When you uncover issues during inspections, this can be an opportunity to negotiate with the seller. While they may not be required to make repairs, you can discuss the possibility of price adjustments or seller credits to address these concerns.

Understanding the Market: Part of "buyer beware" also means understanding the market and the value of the property. Don't overpay for a property that may have significant issues. Ensuring your offer aligns with the market value is a key part of protecting your investment.

"Buyer beware" serves as a reminder that due diligence is paramount in the home buying process. While the "as-is" nature of many transactions simplifies the sale, it emphasizes the need for buyers to approach the process with a keen eye and ensure they are fully informed about the property's condition before finalizing the deal.

CHAPTER 11

Home Inspections and Appraisals

Understanding the significance of home inspections and appraisals is a crucial step in the home-buying process. In this chapter, we explore the purpose of home inspections, how to hire qualified home inspectors, the fundamentals of appraisals, and how to manage low appraisals effectively.

The Purpose of Home Inspections

Home inspections serve several essential purposes in the home-buying process:

1. Identifying Issues: A general home inspection can reveal any issues or defects in the property, helping buyers make informed decisions.

2. Safety Assurance: Inspections ensure the home is safe for habitation, uncovering potential hazards like faulty wiring, structural problems, or environmental issues.

3. Negotiating Power: Inspection results can provide a basis for negotiations with the seller. You may ask them to make repairs or adjust the sale price based on the findings.

Types of Home Inspections to Consider:

1. General Home Inspection: This is a comprehensive assessment of the property's condition, covering structural, electrical, plumbing, and other essential aspects.

2. Termite and Pest Control Inspection: This inspection assesses the presence of termites and other pests, including rodents, ants, and fleas, known for their potential to inflict substantial harm to the property. In some cases, lenders may require termite treatment before the close of escrow. Such treatment may include applying insecticides and eradication or replacement of affected wooden structures around the house, garage, railing, patio posts, or eaves. In more severe instances of infestation, house fumigation (tenting) may be deemed necessary – available options may include traditional gas or organic fumigation products like orange oil. Speak with a professional termite inspector for more information.

3. Roof Inspection: A specialized inspection of the roof's condition, identifying any damage, leaks, or necessary repairs.

4. Septic System Inspection: Relevant for homes with septic systems, this inspection ensures that the system is functioning correctly and not in need of immediate repair or replacement. In some jurisdictions, sellers are required to have the septic system checked and pumped before transferring the property to the new owner.

Hiring a Qualified Home Inspector

Selecting a qualified home inspector is critical. Consider the following factors when choosing an inspector:

1. Credentials and Licensing: Ensure the inspector is certified and licensed, if applicable, in your state. Check for affiliations with professional organizations.

2. Experience: Look for an inspector with substantial experience, preferably in the local housing market.

3. References: Seek recommendations or explore online reviews from previous clients to assess their level of contentment with the inspector's services.

4. Sample Reports: Review sample inspection reports to understand the depth and clarity of their assessments.

5. Cost: Obtain quotes from multiple inspectors and compare their fees.

Understanding Appraisals

Appraisals are a pivotal aspect of the mortgage process. They involve a professional appraiser evaluating the property's market value. Understanding appraisals is essential because they impact your loan.

Appraisal Basics: Appraisers assess the property's condition, location, comparable sales, and other factors to determine its market value.

Lender's Requirement: Lenders will not loan an amount exceeding the appraised value of the property. If the appraisal falls short, you may need to adjust the sale price, cover the difference yourself, or negotiate with the seller.

Handling Low Appraisals

If your home appraisal comes in lower than expected, it's essential to know how to manage the situation:

1. Reevaluation: If you believe the appraisal is inaccurate, you can request a reevaluation or provide additional information to support a higher value. Your real estate agent and the seller's

agent can collaborate to provide supplementary document-tation to the appraiser for reconsideration. Keep in mind that appraisals may occasionally yield lower values, especially for distinctive homes, properties in rural regions, and areas with limited recently sold comparable properties.

2. Negotiation: You can negotiate with the seller to lower the sale price or contribute to covering the difference between the appraised value and the agreed-upon price.

3. Bridge the Gap: In cases of a low appraisal, consider financing options to bridge the gap between the appraised value and the purchase price. Some buyers choose to use their own funds for this purpose. Suppose the gap is relatively small and you intend to stay in the home for an extended period. In that case, there's the possibility that the property's value may appreciate over time, potentially exceeding its purchase price. This long-term perspective can be a strategic decision for those with available funds.

A comprehensive understanding of home inspections and appraisals empowers you to make informed decisions during the home-buying process. It ensures that you are aware of the property's condition and its market value, helping you make strategic choices and negotiate effectively.

CHAPTER 12

The Closing Process

The closing process marks the culmination of your home-buying journey. Although we've mentioned the closing process in previous chapters, in this chapter, we delve into the intricacies of the closing process, including understanding its steps, reviewing the Closing Disclosure, conducting a final walk-through, and signing essential legal documents.

Understanding the Closing Process

The closing process is the final stage, where all necessary steps are completed to transfer the property's ownership from the seller to the buyer. Here are the key aspects to comprehend:

Contingency Removal: By this point of closing the sale, you should have removed contingencies for the investigation and inspection period, the appraisal, and the loan. This step confirms your commitment to the purchase.

Final Walk-Through: Before the closing date, you'll typically conduct a final walk-through to ensure the property is in the agreed-upon condition and that any negotiated repairs have been completed.

Signing Legal Documents: Throughout the closing process, you'll execute a range of legal documents, such as the mortgage note, deed of trust or mortgage, and additional paperwork mandated by the lender and local authorities. A notary may be necessary to validate certain documents.

Reviewing the Closing Documents

The Closing Disclosure is a crucial document you'll receive three days before the closing. It provides a detailed breakdown of the transaction's financial aspects, including:

Loan Terms: The document outlines the loan amount, interest rate, monthly payments, and prepayment penalties.

Closing Costs: It itemizes all closing costs, including fees for the appraisal, title search, attorney's services, and more.

Cash to Close: The Closing Disclosure specifies the amount you need to bring to the closing, which includes the down payment and other costs.

Loan Estimate and Closing Disclosure: Review the Closing Disclosure alongside the Loan Estimate you received earlier to ensure consistency and accuracy.

HUD-1: The document itemizing all the charges paid in connection with the loan at closing.

Final Walk-Through

Before the closing, you have the opportunity to conduct a final walk-through of the property. Here's what to consider during this critical step:

Property Condition: Ensure that the property's condition aligns with what was agreed upon. Verify that any agreed-upon repairs have been made.

Appliances and Systems: Check that all appliances and systems are functioning correctly.

Signing Legal Documents

The closing involves the signing of multiple legal documents, and this can be done in various ways, including electronically, by a mobile notary, or in an office setting. Some of the crucial documents you'll sign include:

Mortgage Note: This is a promise to repay the loan amount to the lender, specifying the interest rate and terms.

Deed of Trust: This legal document grants the lender a security interest in the property, ensuring that the loan is repaid.

Other Required Documents: Depending on local and state regulations, you may need to sign additional disclosures and documents related to the property's transfer.

Understanding the closing process, reviewing all documents and disclosures, conducting a final walk-through, and signing the necessary legal documents are the final steps in acquiring your new home. This section provides a comprehensive overview of the closing process, ensuring you are well-prepared for this significant milestone in your home-buying journey.

CHAPTER 13

Homeownership Responsibilities

Homeownership comes with responsibilities and obligations beyond the excitement of acquiring your new property. In this chapter, we'll explore these responsibilities, including home maintenance, homeowners' associations (HOAs), property taxes, insurance, and handling unexpected repairs.

Home Maintenance

Owning a home means taking care of it to preserve its value and ensure it remains a safe and comfortable place to live. Key aspects of home maintenance include:

Regular Inspections: Periodic inspections of your home, such as checking for leaks, testing smoke detectors, and ensuring proper functioning of appliances and systems, are essential.

Seasonal Maintenance: Consider tasks like cleaning gutters, servicing your HVAC system, and preparing your home for seasonal changes.

Repairs and Upkeep: Be prepared to address minor repairs and general upkeep to prevent larger, costlier issues.

Homeowners Associations (HOA)

In many communities, especially those with shared amenities and common spaces, homeowners' associations play a significant role. HOAs can enforce rules and regulations to maintain a community's appearance and functionality, but they also come with financial obligations, including monthly or annual dues.

HOA Rules and Regulations: Familiarize yourself with the HOA's rules, including any restrictions on property use, exterior modifications, and landscaping.

Financial Commitment: Understand your financial commitment to the HOA, including monthly or annual dues, and budget accordingly.

Meetings and Involvement: Participating in HOA meetings and being an active member can help you stay informed and have a say in community decisions.

Property Taxes and Insurance

Property taxes are a crucial responsibility that homeowners must not neglect. Neglecting to pay property taxes in a timely manner can lead to serious consequences, including liens on the property and foreclosure. Key points regarding property taxes and insurance include:

Property Taxes: Paying property taxes is a legal obligation. Neglecting to do so can result in the county placing a lien on your property or, in severe cases, the property being subject to foreclosure.

Home Insurance: Having adequate homeowners' insurance protects your investment. It covers damage to your property, personal liability, and more. Review your policy thoroughly to ensure it meets your needs.

Handling Unexpected Repairs

Unanticipated repairs can arise at any point in your homeownership journey. Being proactive in handling unexpected expenses is crucial.

Emergency Fund: Consider establishing and maintaining an emergency fund to financially cushion unforeseen repair costs, such as a leaking roof or a malfunctioning HVAC system.

Home Warranty: Deliberate on obtaining a home warranty to provide financial assistance for significant appliances and system repairs. Sellers might include a home warranty, and your agent can assist in incorporating one into your purchase agreement. Acquiring a home warranty is a prudent measure as it can help mitigate expenses related to appliance maintenance, plumbing blockages, or HVAC system repairs. The warranty clearly outlines the scope of covered repairs, ensuring you are well-informed about what to expect.

The Family Trust: Protecting Your Home and Privacy:

Owning a home is more than a financial investment; it's a sanctuary for you and your family. While your home represents security, it's also crucial to ensure its protection extends to your family's privacy and financial well-being. One way to achieve this is by putting your home in a Family Trust.

What is a Family Trust?

A Family Trust, sometimes called a living or revocable trust, is a legal structure responsible for overseeing assets, which can encompass your home to serve the interests of the beneficiaries you've chosen. This trust is established while you're alive and can be adjusted or canceled as circumstances require.

Advantages of a Family Trust:

- Privacy Protection: When your home is held in a Family Trust, it is no longer a matter of public record. The trust owns the property, not you personally, providing a layer of privacy for your family. This can be particularly advantageous if you value confidentiality and wish to shield your family's financial affairs from public scrutiny.

- Estate Planning: Family Trust is a valuable tool for estate planning. It allows you to specify how your assets, including your home, will be distributed upon your passing. This can prevent probate, which is often a lengthy and costly legal process.

- Continuity of Ownership: A Family Trust ensures the smooth transition of ownership. In the event of your passing or incapacity, the trust's successor trustee can manage the property seamlessly, avoiding potential disputes or delays.

- Asset Protection: Family Trusts can protect your home from creditors, lawsuits, or claims that may arise in the future. This safeguards your family's assets and financial security.

- Avoiding Probate: By transferring your home into a Family Trust, you can circumvent the necessity for probate after your passing. Your assets, including your home, will be distributed in accordance with the trust's instructions, streamlining the process for faster and more efficient distribution.

The Process:

1. Establishing the Trust: To create a Family Trust, speak with an attorney who specializes in estate planning.

2. Transferring Ownership: To place your home in the trust, you'll transfer the property's title to the trust. This involves changing the legal ownership of the property, but you retain control and use of your home.

3. Beneficiaries: You'll designate the beneficiaries who will inherit the property or benefit from it during your lifetime. Ensuring Privacy and Peace of Mind:

By utilizing a Family Trust, you not only protect your home but also preserve your family's privacy and financial security. A Family Trust can be especially valuable if you wish to maintain confidentiality, have a clear plan for the future, and avoid probate upon your passing. Consulting with a qualified attorney experienced in estate planning and trust creation is essential to establish a trust tailored to your family's unique needs and circumstances.

Examples of Situations

Family Privacy:
Imagine Sarah, a homeowner who values her family's privacy and wishes to ensure a smooth transition of her home to her children. By establishing a Family Trust, she shields her home from public records, allowing her family to maintain

confidentiality. This trust also outlines her clear intentions for property distribution, avoiding the complexities of probate.

Tax Implications:
Placing your home in a Family Trust can have various tax implications. Speak with a professional tax consultant or attorney to understand the specific tax benefits and considerations in your area. These may include property tax implications, potential reductions in inheritance taxes, and other tax-related aspects that vary depending on your location and the trust's terms.

Success Stories:
The Andersons are a family who, with the guidance of an estate attorney, established a Family Trust. When Mr. Anderson passed away, the trust ensured a seamless transition of ownership to Mrs. Anderson, avoiding disputes or lengthy legal processes. Their story showcases how a Family Trust can provide peace of mind during challenging times.

Common Misconceptions:
Many individuals believe that Family Trusts are overly complex or only applicable to the wealthy. In reality, Family Trusts can be beneficial for a wide range of homeowners and are adaptable to suit various needs. Addressing these misconceptions will help readers understand the practicality and accessibility of this option.

Legal Resources:

Seek out local estate planning attorneys who can provide personalized advice and assistance to help you get started. Additionally, explore online materials and resources that can further educate you on the process. Keep in mind that obtaining professional assistance is essential to customize your trust according to your individual requirements and circumstances.

Disclaimer: Please be aware that no part of this book or this chapter nor the section on Family Trusts constitutes legal advice. Readers are strongly advised and encouraged to seek appropriate legal and professional advice.

CHAPTER 14

Post-Purchase Financial Management

Congratulations on your homeownership! However, the journey doesn't end with the purchase of your home. This chapter delves into the crucial aspects of managing your finances after buying a home, including budgeting, building home equity, exploring refinancing options, and long-term financial planning.

Budgeting After Homeownership

- Owning a home introduces a new set of financial responsibilities. Budgeting is vital to maintaining a stable financial future:

- Updated Budget: Review and update your budget to include mortgage payments, property taxes, insurance, and home maintenance costs. Be thorough in accounting for these new expenses.

- Emergency Fund: Maintain an emergency fund for unexpected repairs and other homeownership-related expenses.

- Utility Costs: Expect changes in utility costs compared to when you were renting. Heating, cooling, and general maintenance may differ in a house.

- Home Improvement: Plan for home improvement projects and renovations. Homeownership allows you to customize your space, but it's essential to budget for these enhancements.

Building Home Equity

Homeownership offers a unique advantage: the opportunity to build equity over time. Equity represents the gap between the market value of your home and your outstanding mortgage balance. Here's how you can build equity:

- Regular Mortgage Payments: As you make regular mortgage payments, you gradually reduce the principal balance. This builds your equity.

- Property Value Appreciation: Over time, your property may appreciate in value due to market conditions or improvements you make.

- Shorter Mortgage Terms: Opting for a shorter mortgage term can help you build equity faster.

- Leverage Home Improvements: Renovations that add value to your home can increase your equity.

Refinancing Options

Refinancing your mortgage can be valuable for optimizing your financial situation. Consider these scenarios for refinancing:

- Lower Interest Rates: If interest rates have declined since you took out your original loan, refinancing can lead to lower monthly payments.

- Shorter Loan Term: Refinancing into a shorter-term mortgage can help you pay off your home faster and save on interest.

- Cash-Out Refinancing: You can access your home's equity through a cash-out refinance, which can be used for other financial goals.

- Debt Consolidation: Roll high-interest debt into your mortgage by opting for a cash-out refinance to simplify payments and reduce interest costs.

- Home Improvement: Use a cash-out refinance to fund home improvements that can increase your property's value.

Long-Term Financial Planning

Owning a home is a significant step in your long-term financial plan. Consider these aspects for a secure financial future:

- Retirement Planning: Continue or initiate retirement savings to ensure a comfortable retirement.

- Estate Planning: Update your estate plan to reflect your new homeownership and any changes in your financial situation.

- Investments: Diversify your investments to include both real estate and other assets.

- Review Financial Goals: Regularly review your financial goals and make adjustments as needed.

Owning a home is a financial commitment, but it also provides opportunities to build wealth through home equity and long-term financial planning. With a well-managed budget, an eye on equity growth, the potential for refinancing, and a clear long-term financial plan, you can enjoy the many financial benefits of homeownership while securing your future financial well-being.

CHAPTER 15

Bonus Tips and Resources

In this section we provide some additional insights and resources to further enhance your home buying experience. Here, we delve into negotiation strategies, red flags to be aware of, the potential to turn your new home into a source of profit, frequently asked questions, and provide you with an array of additional resources to support your homeownership journey.

Negotiation Strategies

Negotiation is a critical element of the home buying process. Advanced negotiation strategies that can give you an edge when making an offer. Here's how to do it:

1. Position Yourself as a Strong Buyer: Showcase your commitment and readiness to buy by being pre-approved for a mortgage and having your finances in order. This positions you as a serious contender in negotiations.

2. Identify Your Priorities: Clearly define what aspects of the deal matter most to you. Is it the purchase price, contingencies, or specific repair requests? Knowing your priorities allows you to focus your negotiation efforts effectively.

3. Offer with Confidence: Craft an offer that reflects your priorities while respecting the seller's position. Show enthusiasm but remain within your budget and be prepared to justify your offer.

4. Request Repairs and Adjustments: If the home inspection reveals issues, request repairs or price adjustments as needed. Communicate your concerns clearly and professionally.

5. Know When to Walk Away: Sometimes, it's in your best interest to walk away from a deal if the terms are not favorable or if there are too many repairs that will cause a financial strain on your budget. Trust your instincts and be prepared to explore other options.

Red Flags to Watch Out For

When purchasing a home, it's essential to be vigilant and identify potential red flags that could signal problems with a property or the transaction. Here's how to do it:

1. Conduct a Thorough Inspection: Hire a qualified home inspector to examine the property thoroughly. Pay attention to their findings, and don't hesitate to ask questions.

2. Research the Neighborhood: Investigate the neighborhood for potential issues like crime rates, traffic, and proximity to amenities. Visit at different times of the day to get a comprehensive feel for the area.

3. Review Documentation Carefully: It is extremely crucial to scrutinize all documents, contracts, and disclosures related to the transaction. Failure to do so may leave you with a property you regret purchasing. Buying property is not the same as buying a toaster where you can return it to the store if there's a malfunction. Ask questions and or seek legal advice if necessary to ensure you fully understand the terms and implications.

4. Consult Experts: When in doubt, consult professionals, such as real estate agents, lawyers, or contractors, who can provide guidance and expertise to address your concerns.

Unlocking Your New Home's Financial Potential

Your new home is more than just a residence; it's a potential source of profit. Discover strategic ways to turn your property into a lucrative asset:

1. Leverage Additional Space: If your home boasts extra rooms or a separate unit, consider renting it out to tenants or through short-term traveler platforms. This can create a reliable stream of rental income. Extend your hospitality to essential workers like nurses or doctors, international students, and professionals like executives for added earning potential.

2. Strategic Investments for Value Boost: Elevate your home's worth and equity by investing strategically in improvements. Renovations, energy-efficient upgrades,

and landscaping enhancements contribute to a higher resale value.

3. Solar Power for Sustainable Profits: Install solar panels not just to save on energy costs but also to potentially sell surplus energy back to the local electric company. This can lead to additional credits and household income, transforming your home into an eco-friendly profit center.

4. ADU Exploration for Added Income: Research local regulations, including Senate Bill 9 (SB-9), to explore the potential of building Accessory Dwelling Units (ADUs). Whether in your backyard, above the garage, or as a garage conversion, ADUs can provide rental income or accommodate extended family. Ensure compliance with building regulations and permits before proceeding, as building without permits may seem cost-effective upfront but can impact your resale value.

Unlock the financial potential of your property with due diligence. Research local laws, consult legal advisors, engage with general contractors for building regulations, and check rental restrictions or permits before embarking on transformative projects. This strategic approach contributes to securing your financial future.

Protecting Your New Home

1. Install a Home Security System

A holistic security system ensures the safeguarding of your property through:

Alarms: Strategically placed alarms serve as a powerful deterrent, effectively alerting both you and your neighbors to potential intruders.

Cameras: Real-time monitoring and recording capabilities provide crucial evidence in case of incidents, enhancing overall security and surveillance.

Sensors: Motion sensors, strategically placed, detect any movement around your property, triggering immediate alerts for heightened security awareness.

2. Doorbell Cameras

Modern security is elevated with doorbell cameras, offering:

Enhanced Security: Monitor and record visitors at your doorstep, deter package theft and provide documented evidence of any suspicious activities.

Remote Monitoring: Access live footage and receive alerts remotely, providing an added layer of security even when you're away from home.

3. Outdoor Lighting

Well-lit exteriors significantly contribute to overall home security:

Visibility: Adequate lighting eliminates hiding spots, discouraging unauthorized access by enhancing visibility around your property.

Safety: Illuminated pathways and entrances not only enhance safety for residents and visitors but also contribute to the overall security of your home.

4. Secure Entry Points

Reinforce your home's entry points for enhanced security:

Rekeying Locks and Reprogramming Remotes: Invest in getting all entry points rekeyed including reprogramming any remote controls, such as, garage remotes. A good home warranty plan will offer special discounts for rekeying your new home.

Sturdy Locks: Investing in high-quality locks for doors and windows adds an extra layer of protection, bolstering the security of your home.

Deadbolts: The installation of deadbolts reinforces doors, making access more challenging for potential intruders.

Smart Locks: Upgrading to smart locks adds convenience and allows for remote control and access management, enhancing overall security.

5. Neighborhood Watch

Participating in or establishing a neighborhood watch program promotes a sense of community and overall safety:

Community Unity: Collaborative efforts with neighbors foster a watchful eye on the neighborhood, creating a sense of community and shared responsibility.

Timely Reporting: Prompt reporting of suspicious activities to local authorities contributes to a safer community, ensuring that potential security threats are addressed promptly.

By implementing these measures, you secure your property and actively contribute to your neighborhood's safety. A proactive approach to home security ensures peace of mind for you and your family, establishing a secure foundation for a thriving community.

Frequently Asked Questions

As a homebuyer, you're bound to have questions and uncertainties along the way. We've compiled a list of frequently asked questions to provide you with quick and accessible answers.

How much should I budget for a down payment on a home?
- Answer: The recommended down payment is typically 20% of the home's purchase price. However, there are various lenders who may require far less, 5% to 10%. Loan programs exist that require lower down payments, such as FHA loans with as little as 3.5% down, VA loans with no down payment for eligible veterans, and USDA loans with no down payment for rural and suburban

areas. It's essential to consider your financial situation and loan options to determine the right down payment for you. Each lender is different and down payment requirements will vary. Shop around for at least three quotes and go with the one that best fits your situation.

What's the difference between a fixed-rate and adjustable-rate mortgage?

- Answer: A fixed-rate mortgage has a stable interest rate that doesn't change over the life of the loan, providing predictable monthly payments. In contrast, an adjustable-rate mortgage (ARM) has an initial fixed-rate period, after which the interest rate adjusts periodically based on market conditions. ARMs typically offer lower initial interest rates but come with the potential for increased payments in the future.

How do I calculate the total cost of homeownership, including taxes and insurance?

- Answer: To calculate your total monthly housing expenses, add your mortgage principal and interest, property taxes, homeowner's insurance, and, if applicable, private mortgage insurance (PMI). It's crucial to factor in all these costs to determine the affordability of your new home.

What is a closing disclosure, and why is it important?

- Answer: A closing disclosure is a detailed document provided by your lender at least three days before closing. It outlines the final terms of your mortgage, including interest rates, monthly payments, closing costs, and any cash you need to bring to the closing. Review it carefully to ensure accuracy and understand the financial implications of your mortgage.

What contingencies should I include in my purchase agreement?

- Answer: Common contingencies include inspection, financing, and appraisal contingencies. These provisions allow you to inspect the property, secure financing, and ensure the home's appraised value aligns with your offer. Including contingencies can protect you from unforeseen issues and provide opportunities to negotiate or walk away if necessary.

To further support your pursuit of homeownership, we've gathered a comprehensive list of additional resources at the end of this book. These resources include website references, and organizations that can provide in-depth information, tools, and services to assist you in your home buying process.

In conclusion, armed with negotiation skills, a keen eye for red flags, financial strategies, answers to common questions, and an extensive list of valuable resources, you'll be well-equipped to make the most of your home buying journey. Let this book serve as a valuable guide to enhance your overall home buying experience and empower you with the knowledge and tools necessary to succeed in the real estate market.

CHAPTER 16

Summary and Conclusion

In this comprehensive guide to buying a home, we have explored a journey to empower you with the knowledge and tools necessary for a successful homeownership experience. Throughout the chapters, we've covered every facet of the home buying process, offering insights and guidance at every turn.

We started by laying the essential financial foundations, ensuring you are well-prepared for the path ahead. From improving your credit to saving for a down payment, these critical steps set the stage for a successful home purchase.

As we continued, we explored the intricacies of mortgages, shedding light on the various types, pre-approval, interest rates, and mortgage closing costs. Armed with this knowledge, you gained the confidence to choose the right mortgage that aligns with your unique financial situation.

Our journey led us through effective house-hunting strategies, home tours, and the art of negotiation. You learned to craft strong offers and navigate complex contracts, setting the stage for a successful transaction.

Home inspections and appraisals were demystified, allowing you to identify red flags and understand their importance. The closing process, from reviewing the closing disclosure to signing legal documents, was explained, ensuring a smooth transition to homeownership.

Responsibilities that come with homeownership were addressed, emphasizing the significance of home maintenance, understanding homeowners' associations, and the critical nature of property taxes and insurance. Post-purchase financial management, including budgeting, building home equity, and long-term financial planning, provided you with the tools to thrive as a responsible homeowner.

We expanded your horizons by showcasing unconventional paths to homeownership. Each method offers a unique approach, and understanding these options can be invaluable for buyers seeking unconventional paths to property ownership.

Further, we've incorporated additional resources, links to down payment assistance, including home buyer calculators, to further assist you in your home buying journey. These tools are designed to provide practical assistance in your financial planning and decision-making.

In conclusion, this guide is your comprehensive reference, arming you with the knowledge and tools necessary for a successful and rewarding homeownership experience. Whether you're a first-time homebuyer or an experienced one, we hope this guide has been a valuable resource, empowering you to make informed and confident decisions throughout your home buying journey.

We encourage you to seek professional guidance when needed and remember that a skilled real estate agent can be your dependable partner, offering support and guidance at every stage of the process. We wish you the best of luck in your pursuit of homeownership, and may your new home bring you joy, comfort, and financial security for years to come. Happy house hunting, and best wishes for your future endeavors!

ADDITIONAL RESOURCES & LINKS

Loan Type Recap:

Conventional – A conventional mortgage can lead to a fixed rate or adjustable rate for your primary home, secondary home, or investment property. These types of loans are more flexible and not guaranteed or insured by the government. For conventional loans with less than 20% down may incur private mortgage insurance (PMI). Conventional loans are great for those with good to excellent credit.

FHA – An FHA mortgage is a great program for buyers. It's advantages are a low down payment without private mortgage insurance (PMI). FHA loans tend to be a little higher due to mortgage insurance premiums (MIP). FHA loans are insured and backed by government agencies (Federal Housing Administration).

VA – Specific for Veterans and surviving spouse of a veteran. A VA Mortgage offers many benefits, including no down payment and lower interest rates.

USDA – These are only available in certain areas deemed rural by the United States Department of Agriculture. Surprisingly, many properties on the outskirts of a metro area will qualify for these loan programs, including large a plot of land with a farmhouse. The advantages of a USDA Mortgage are lower interest rates and zero down payment.

LOAN QUALIFICATIONS CRITERIA

Conventional Loans
Conventional 97
FICO score 620
DTI (Debt To Income Ratio) 43%
Allows buyer 3% to 20% down depending on the price of the home
Jumbo loans available (loan amounts above loan limits)

FHA Home Loans https://www.hud.gov/buying/loans
FICO Score as low as 600
DTI (Debt To Income Ratio) up to 50%
Allows buyer 3.5% down
Allows for 2nd time home buyer
Higher income allowed
No restrictions on areas where borrowers can purchase
Refinancing available

FHA 203k Rehab allows for repairs and new construction.
- Streamline FHA 203k allows up to $38,000 and you can do the work yourself
- Standard FHA203k allows more rehab but process takes more paperwork and time

USDA Loans   https://eligibility.sc.egov.usda.gov
FICO Score as low as 620
$0 down payment
100% financing available
Only in eligible areas – Area restrictions apply
Allows for Single Family Home 1 unit

- USDA 502 Guaranteed _ allows for higher income
- USDA 502 Direct Loan _ allows for lower income

VA Home Loans - https://www.va.gov/housing-assistance/home-loans/eligibility/
- No FICO Score limit (some lenders require 620)
- $0 down payment
- Cash Out Refinance
- Surviving spouse eligible
- Need Certificate of Eligibility (COE)
- Benefits can be used multiple times
- Native American Direct Loan (NADL) Program

Disclaimer: Consumers are encouraged to consult with a lender to verify eligibility and qualifications required.

DOWN PAYMENT ASSISTANCE PROGRAMS

Governmental down payment assistance programs can be your first source to investigate for available funds. However, be aware that some programs run out of money very quickly due to high demand. You will also want to research for private, local state, county, and city in which you plan to purchase your home because down payment assistance programs may be available.

Pros and Cons of Down Payment Assistance Program

Pros:

1. Increased Affordability: Down payment assistance programs can make homeownership more accessible by providing financial support for the initial purchase costs.

2. Expanded Home Options: With assistance, buyers may qualify for a higher loan amount, broadening their options and potentially allowing them to consider homes in a higher price range.

3. Financial Flexibility: Buyers can use their savings for other purposes, such as emergency funds, home improvements, or investments, as the down payment assistance covers a significant portion of the upfront costs.

4. Potential for Lower Interest Rates: Some down payment assistance programs offer favorable interest rates, reducing the overall cost of the mortgage for the buyer.

5. Path to Homeownership: For those struggling to save a large sum for a down payment, these programs provide a viable path to homeownership.

Cons:

1. Income Limits: Many down payment assistance programs have income restrictions, limiting eligibility for higher-income individuals or families.

2. Property Restrictions: Some programs may have restrictions on the type or location of the property, potentially limiting the buyer's choices.

3. Resale Restrictions: Certain programs may impose resale restrictions, requiring the buyer to stay in the home for a specified period before selling.

4. Complex Application Process: The application process for down payment assistance programs can be complex and time-consuming, requiring thorough documentation and adherence to specific guidelines.

5. Limited Availability: These programs may have limited funding or be subject to changes in government policies, leading to uncertainties about their continued availability.

6. Potential for Higher Monthly Payments: In some cases, down payment assistance may result in higher monthly mortgage payments or additional fees, depending on the terms of the assistance.

7. Cost of Assistance: Some down payment assistance programs may come with additional costs, such as origination fees or higher interest rates. These costs can add up over the life of the mortgage.

8. Repayment Obligations: In certain programs, the assistance provided is structured as a loan that needs to be repaid. This could impact the buyer's ability to sell the home in the future, as they may be required to pay back the assistance upon resale.

It's crucial for buyers to thoroughly review the terms and conditions of any down payment assistance program they consider and carefully assess the potential long-term implications on their financial situation and homeownership journey.

Buyers considering down payment assistance should carefully weigh these factors, considering their financial situation, long-term plans, and the specific terms of the assistance program.

LIST OF DOWN PAYMENT PROGRAMS

CalHFA (Calif HFA) Check your local HFA programs
FICO Score at least 640
CALHFA has several down payment assistant programs.
For details visit: https://www.calhfa.ca.gov/index.htm

CalHFA Forgivable Equity Builder loan first time buyer:
https://www.calhfa.ca.gov/homebuyer/programs/forgivable.
htm

GSFA – Golden State Finance Authority
These loan programs offer with a 3% to 7% grant
No restrictions on the area borrowers can purchase. Grant can
be used to cover down payment and closing costs can be
structured both as FHA and Conventional. Calif program.
For details visit: http://www.gsfahome.org

HUD Programs
https://www.hud.gov/states/california/homeownership/buyi
ngprgms

Neighborhood Partnership Housing Services (NPHS)
California program. For details visit: **www.nphsinc.org**

Neighborhood Assistance Corporation of America
NACA is a nationwide non-government, non-profit
organization who helps homebuyers prepare for homeownership. Program offers 100% financing.
For details visit: **www.naca.com**

For additional Down Payment Resources visit:
http://bit.ly/DPA_Calif or Scan QR Code Below

HOME BUYER READINESS CHECKLIST

1. Make sure you are ready

☐ You have a stable job/income.

☐ You can see yourself living in the same town for the next five to ten years.

☐ You are prepared for the extra work that comes with homeownership.

2. Create your wish list

☐ Use the handy chart below to determine what is most important to have right now (e.g. location, number of beds, yard, etc.).

☐ Check out different neighborhoods, home styles and listings online to get a feel for what is most important to you.

3. Figure out your budget

☐ Request your credit report from all three credit bureaus (Equifax, Experian, and TransUnion). Fix any errors right away.

☐ Determine a down payment amount (ideally 3-20% to avoid paying private mortgage insurance).

☐ Calculate how much you will need in an emergency fund (for unexpected maintenance or repair costs).

4. Gather necessary documents

☐ Collect proof of employment, including pay stubs and past tax returns.

☐ Print our bank and investment account statements from the past 30 days.

☐ Compile your previous addresses and current landlords contact information.

5. **Research mortgages**

☐ Request quotes from multiple lenders and comparison shop for loans.

☐ Get pre-qualified for a loan to rank your buying power

☐ Once you've submitted all required documents to your lender, obtain a copy of your pre-approval letter.

☐ Be prepared to share a copy of your preapproval letter with your agent. Agents will not take you to view homes without you having a lenders pre-approval letter and showing proof of funds. In some areas, sellers may request a copy of your pre-approval letter or proof of funding before allowing you to view their home.

6. **Assemble your team**

☐ Now that you have secured and established your means of purchasing your home, get started in finding your new home.

WHAT TO EXPXECT DURING A HOME SALE

General Checklist

Process may differ based on jurisdiction

- ❑ **Initial Meeting**
  - Determine needs and wants
  - Determine financial eligibility
  - Sign Partnership Agreement with your Realtor

- ❑ **Loan Qualification with Lender**
  - Discuss finances
  - Provide lender with financial documents
  - Obtain preapproval letter from lender (Must do this before looking for homes)

- ❑ **Find a Home**
  - Provide agent with copy of preapproval letter and proof of funds
  - Select an affordable property that fits your needs
  - Discuss offer with agent
  - Buyer reviews contract with agent
  - Agent presents offer to sellers

- ❑ **Present and Negotiate Offer**
  - Seller reviews offer (Seller can accept, counter, or reject your offer)
  - Buyer prepares "earnest money" deposit (typically, 3% of purchase price)

- ❑ **Open Escrow After Offer is Accepted**

- 3 days after offer is accepted, deposit "earnest money" into escrow
- Escrow will order Preliminary Report
- Sign and submit all required documents

❑ **Contingency Period**
- Conduct Inspections- general, termite, roofing, etc by a qualified professional
- Review and sign all seller transfer disclosures
- Review and sign Preliminary Report
- Conduct property appraisal – ordered by the lender
- Finalize loan underwriting and prepare all down payment
- Remove all contingencies once satisfied with inspections and loan is approved

❑ **Obtain Homeowners Insurance**
- Select insurance company and coverage
- Insurance will be in effect at close of escrow

❑ **Home Warranty / NHD Report, if applicable**
- Review and Sign Documents, if applicable

❑ **Review Escrow Documents**
- Review itemized summary of closing costs (HUD-1)
- Sign required loan documents
- Title Vesting, determine how you want to take title
- Down payment ready for bank wire or cashier's check prior to closing date

❑ **Closing the Escrow**
- Conduct final walk through at least 5 days before closing
- Deposit down payment and closing costs
- Lender sends funds to designated Title company
- Deed is recorded with County Recorder's office
- Get your keys and move in! – Keys are typically given to buyer once the recording has been confirmed

SERVICE PROVIDERS

Search online for service providers you'll need during your home search, and post purchase. Your real estate agent may also provide a list of recommended vendors with special deals. The list below comprises commonly known online resources for your convenience and does not imply affiliation or recommendations. Prior to engaging with any service provider, it is essential to conduct independent research. The inclusion of a company on this list does not guarantee or endorse its services. Users are responsible for verifying the credibility, reliability, and suitability of any service provider. This list is for informational purposes only, and users should exercise caution and diligence in their decision-making.

1. Local Information and Reviews:

- Google: An extensive search engine for local businesses and services.
- Yelp: A platform for customer reviews and ratings on various businesses and services.
- Yahoo: Provides search results and local information, including reviews.

2. Neighborhood Information:

- Bestplaces.net: Offers information on cities, neighborhoods, and various demographics.
- Areavibes.com: Provides livability scores and neighborhood information.
- City-data.com: Offers comprehensive data on cities, including demographics and crime rates.
- Greatschools.com: Evaluates and rates schools in different areas.

- Neighborhood Scout (neighborhoodscout.com): Research neighborhood statistics and compare areas.
- Crimereports.com: Access crime data for better neighborhood understanding.

3. Home Improvement and Maintenance:
- Houzz: A platform for home design and remodeling ideas.
- HomeAdvisor (homeadvisor.com): Get quotes from local contractors for home improvement projects.
- Thumbtack (thumbtack.com): Find local professionals for various home services.
- Empire Today Flooring: Provides flooring and installation services in 24 hours.

4. Moving and Storage Solutions:
- Movers.com: Connects users with moving companies and services.
- Precision Movers: A reliable moving company.
- Pods.com: Offers portable storage solutions.
- Storageunits.com: Helps find local storage facilities.
- Lifestorage.com: Provides storage solutions.
- U-Haul (uhaul.com): Explore options for truck rentals and moving supplies.

5. Insurance Providers:
- Homesite Insurance: Offers homeowners insurance.
- Esurance: Provides insurance services.
- Steadily Insurance: Offers insurance solutions nationwide.

- USAA Insurance: Specializes in insurance for military personnel.
- New York Life Mortgage Insurance: Provides mortgage life insurance.
- Farmers Insurance: Comprehensive insurance coverage.
- Nationwide Insurance: Offers a variety of insurance products.
- State Farm Insurance: Provides insurance services and financial planning.

6. Credit and Financial Information:

- CreditKarma.com: Provides credit scores and financial insights.
- AnnualCreditReport.com: Allows free annual credit reports.
- Creditrepair.com: Offers credit repair services.
- Experian.com: Provides credit reports and scores.
- NerdWallet (nerdwallet.com): Access tools and advice for financial planning.

7. Mortgage and Financing:

- Geneva Financial: Mortgage and financing services.
- Veterans United: Specialized in VA home loans.
- Trade Mark Financing: Offers financing solutions.
- RWM Loans: Provides mortgage and home loan services.
- America Mortgages Foreign National Loans: Offers mortgage services for foreign nationals.
- Guaranteed Rate Loans: Mortgage and home loan services.

8. Government Resources:

- HUD.gov: U.S. Department of Housing and Urban Development for housing resources.
- FHFA.gov: Federal Housing Finance Agency for housing and mortgage information.
- USDA.gov: U.S. Department of Agriculture for rural development programs.

9. Home Security:
- ADT Safe Haven Home Security: Offers comprehensive home security solutions.
- SimpliSafe (simplisafe.com): Explore options for DIY home security systems.

10. Home Inspection Services:
- InterNACHI (internachi.org): The International Association of Certified Home Inspectors provides a directory of certified inspectors.
- PillarToPost Home Inspectors: Professional home inspection services.
- Terminix (terminix.com): Pest control and termite inspection services.
- Networx (networx.com): Connect with qualified pest control and home termite inspectors.

11. Solar Power Providers:
- Apricot Solar: Offers solar power solutions.
- SunPower Solar: Provides solar energy services.
- EnergyStar (energystar.gov): Learn about energy-efficient products and practices for your home.

12. Real Estate Auction Platforms:

- Auction.com: Online real estate auction platform.
- Bid4Assets: Another platform for online real estate auctions.
- Realtybid.com: Specialized in real estate auctions.
- Xome.com: Online real estate auction platform for buying and selling services.
- Hubzu: Online real estate auction platform for buying and selling homes.

13. Home Warranty and Insurance:

- Fidelity Home Warranty: Offers comprehensive home warranty services.
- First American Home Warranty: Provides home warranty services.
- American Shield Home Warranty: Comprehensive home warranty coverage.

14. Utility Providers:

- Utility Score (utilityscore.com): Evaluate utility costs and providers for specific properties.

15. Legal Services:

- Avvo (avvo.com): Connect with lawyers and read reviews to find the right legal assistance.
- Legal Match (legalmatch.com): Connect with experienced attorneys for legal advice.

MOVING CHECKLIST
Start Planning Your Move Now

Moving to a new home can be an exciting but often challenging experience. To help you stay organized and reduce stress during the moving process, we've compiled this comprehensive checklist. Use it to plan and manage your move efficiently.

Before You Move:

1. Create a Moving Binder: Start by setting up a dedicated folder or binder to keep all your moving-related documents, receipts, and notes in one place.

2. Declutter: Go through your belongings and decide what to keep, donate, sell, or discard. The less you move, the easier the process.

3. Set a Moving Date: Determine your moving day and book your moving company or rental truck well in advance.

4. Notify Utility Providers: Contact your current and future utility providers (electricity, water, gas, internet, etc.) to schedule the transfer or setup of services.

5. Change of Address: Update your address with the post office, banks, credit card companies, and any other relevant institutions.

6. Notify Subscriptions: Inform magazine subscriptions, online retailers, and other services about your change of address.

7. Packing Supplies: Gather packing materials, including boxes, bubble wrap, packing tape, and markers. Start packing non-essential items early.

8. Label Boxes: Label each box with its contents and the room it should go to in your new home.

Moving Day:

1. Final Walkthrough: Do a final walkthrough of your old home to ensure you haven't left anything behind.

2. Pack an Essentials Box: Prepare a box with essential items like toiletries, a change of clothes, and important documents to keep with you during the move.

3. Inventory List: Keep an inventory of your possessions as you load them onto the moving truck.

4. Supervise the Move: If you're using a moving company, be present to oversee the loading and unloading of your belongings.

Upon Arrival:

1. Unpack Essentials First: Start with the essentials box and gradually unpack room by room.

2. Inspect Your Belongings: Check for any damage or missing items and document them if necessary.

3. Connect Utilities: Ensure all utilities are connected and working in your new home.

4. Explore the Neighborhood: Familiarize yourself with your new neighborhood, locate nearby amenities, and introduce yourself to neighbors.

Within the First Week:

1. Child and Pet Care: If you have children or pets, ensure they are comfortable and safe in their new environment.

2. Organize and Decorate: Start organizing your belongings and decorating your new home according to your preferences.

3. Update Documents: Visit your local DMV to update your driver's license and vehicle registration if you've moved to a new state.

4. Emergency Services: Find the nearest hospitals, fire stations, and police stations in your area.

Additional Resources:

1. Local Services: Research local service providers, such as healthcare, schools, and grocery stores.

2. Home Maintenance: Familiarize yourself with home maintenance tasks and schedules specific to your new location.

4. Community Involvement: Discover local community organizations, events, and groups to get involved in.

5. Safety Precautions: Implement safety measures, like installing smoke detectors and securing doors and windows.

6. Get to Know Neighbors: Establish connections with your neighbors; a friendly community can make your new place feel like home.

Moving can be a significant life change, but with careful planning and organization, it can be a smooth and enjoyable transition. Use this checklist to keep track of essential tasks and ensure a successful move to your new home.

About the Author

Toi Holliday is a dedicated real estate professional with over two decades of experience in the client service industry. Her comprehensive background encompasses various facets of real estate, from investment and traditional sales to short-sale foreclosures, probate, trusts, land transactions, vacant properties, distressed, and tax-delinquent properties. This extensive experience equips her with a detailed understanding of the intricacies of real estate transactions.

Toi is the author of Maximizing Your Vacant Property, Home Selling Secrets Unveiled, Complete Guide to Buying a Home and several other educational resource guides offering vital insights for successfully navigating the real estate process. Through her written guidance, she empowers sellers and buyers to make informed decisions in their real estate journey.

Committed to excellence, Toi combines her passion for assisting people with her expertise to create a comprehensive approach to serving a diverse clientele.

As a REALTOR® based in Los Angeles, California, Toi is active in her communities and holds memberships in various local and global associations. She enjoys spending time with her family and friends in her spare time, hiking, and traveling.

For more information about the author, visit:
www.ToiHolliday.com
CalDRE# 02018834

Scan Here

www.ingramcontent.com/pod-product-compliance
Lightning Source LLC
Chambersburg PA
CBHW070019300526
45794CB00001B/367